THE LITERATURE TOOLBOX

THE LITERATURE TOOLBOX

Practical Strategies for Exploring Texts

GLEN PEARSALL

*To my Mum whose love of reading
and to my Dad whose struggle with it
inspired me to be an English teacher…*

© Glen Pearsall 2024

First published in 2014 by TLN Press
Republished in 2020 by Hawker Brownlow Education
This edition published in 2024 by Amba Press

Editor: Natasha Harris

All rights reserved. No part of this book may be reproduced or transmitted in any form or by any means, electronic or mechanical, including photocopying, recording or by any information storage and retrieval system, without prior permission in writing from the publisher.

Published by Amba Press
Melbourne, Australia
www.ambapress.com.au

ISBN: 9781923116511 (pbk)
ISBN: 9781923116528 (ebk)

A catalogue record for this book is available from the National Library of Australia.

Contents

Introduction	1
Chapter One: Creating Engaged Readers	3
Encountering Text	6
Unpacking a Sentence	7
Three-Colour Highlighting	8
Replacement Tasks	10
The Connotations Game	12
Taking Note	13
Open-Book Index Challenge	14
Cue Sheets	16
Split-Page Analysis	18
See, Think and Wonder	20
Silent Screen/Blank Screen	21
Conducting Classroom Discussions	22
The Top Ten Strategic Questioning Toolkit	23
Distant Reading	27
Word Clouds	28
Ngram Viewer	31
Appendix: Code Words	32

Chapter Two: Working Faster, Reading Deeper	35
Foundation Knowledge	38
Sequence Strips	39
Instant Picture Book	40
Race the Bell	41
Synthesis Tasks	42
Testing Foundation Knowledge	44
Four Tell	45
The Up and Down Game	46
Reading Deeper	47
Reading Process Reports	48
Prompt Generator	50
Line Debating	52
Developing Understanding	54
Character Ranking	55
Hidden Thoughts	56
Role-play Activities	58
Critical Material Auction	61
Non-linguistic Representations	62

Chapter Three: Getting it in Writing	**65**
Refining Essay Technique	68
Bundling Swap	69
Quotation Strips	70
The Plot Box	72
Support-Challenge Continuum	73
Inverse Models	74
Editing Yahtzee	76
Sixteens	77
Practising Prose	78
Linking Game	79
Grouping Evidence	80
Developed Reading	82
Comparing Pieces of Writing	84
However-ing	86
Line Length Activities	87
Woven Quotes	88
Mastery Grid	90
About the Author	**93**
References	**95**
Index	**97**

Introduction

The most successful English students demonstrate a 'fullness of response'.

They read closely, immersing themselves in the text. They grant characters the complexity of their own motivations. Successful English students wrestle with meaning. They tease out tensions and contradictions in a text, constantly revisiting and revising their views. Successful English students don't just do the work. They learn and grow from it.

Expert teachers understand that this is a slow process. They remember that first readings can be bewildering or enchanting and leave space in their curriculum for the tentative process of reading and re-reading. They then help their students connect this private experience to the wider world. Expert teachers introduce students to other voices and other lives ... and in doing so, help students find their own voices.

Anyone who has taught Elizabethan drama to a class of distracted teenagers knows that this can be challenging work. Just helping students to learn to read—or, once they can read, read the book—can be an enormous task. But it is a deeply rewarding one.

This text offers teachers practical, classroom-tested techniques for realising these challenging goals. It is organised into three chapters:

- Chapter 1 argues that teaching students to write well about literature is often a matter of teaching students to read well.
- Chapter 2 suggests that if we are to do this effectively we need strategies for reducing the amount of time devoted to teaching foundation knowledge so we can use this additional class time to elicit more sophisticated readings.
- Chapter 3 offers strategies for improving specific aspects of student writing about literature.

This focus on practising specific skills is not to be confused with more formulaic approaches to teaching English classes. In *The Literature Toolbox,* I won't explore pro-forma essay structures or advocate any single instructional strategy as the sole way to approach a problem. Rather than teaching students to copy narrow recipes for success, I believe we must show students that achievement involves steadily building up a bank of skills and strategies with which to examine and respond to literature in their own voices. Students need to learn that a successful response is not the result of natural flair, but something that is *made*. Excellence can be built.

Literature, then, is not something we learn: it is something we do.

> Expert teachers introduce students to other voices and other lives ... and in doing so, help students find their own voices.

Chapter 1

CREATING ENGAGED READERS

Exploring Text and Fostering Engagement

Great writing is a product of great reading. To improve our students' writing about literature we must focus primarily on teaching students how to become better readers. Indeed, much of the discussion about the strengths and limitations of student *writing* should actually refer to the skills and knowledge that can best be developed through effective classroom *reading*.

If we want our students to produce cohesive and fluent written responses, we must first teach them to become literate readers. Critical reading is a complex, high-order skill, but it is possible to identify the traits that are most closely associated with its development. These traits are often grouped under the label 'performative literacy' (Blau, 2003). Highly accomplished readers:

- are capable of sustained, focused attention and demonstrate a willingness to suspend closure
- have a capacity for intellectual risk taking and are prepared to take chances and make mistakes
- understand knowledge as conditional and, while they are ready to 'make a case' for their point of view, they can also change their mind
- demonstrate metacognition, monitoring the extent of their learning in an ongoing way.

The first two chapters of this resource explore strategies for creating this kind of open, reflective approach to reading in our English classes. In this first chapter we consider simple strategies for fostering engagement in readers. We discuss techniques for teaching young people to observe closely, draw inferences and then carefully record their insights. We explore strategies for finding pathways into difficult or dry material and for making use of prior knowledge and learning. We offer techniques for creating a classroom culture where students readily identify and discuss the limits of their understanding.

Close, engaged reading is central to effective student practice. Without this basic engagement with text, all other elements of an English teacher's craft are moot. If students won't read the book or report honestly about the limits of their knowledge, then the best delivered lesson in the world is just filler between recess and lunchtime.

Encountering Text

The best activities for unpacking a new text not only help students develop better textual knowledge but also signal the kind of approaches required to make the most of that knowledge.

These signals are crucial. Students who underperform in English often do so because, at a fundamental level, they misunderstand what is required of them. They paraphrase, for instance, instead of analysing texts. They identify quotes without weighing their meaning or significance. They think that their goal is immediate mastery rather than persistent investigation. In these instances, students aren't so much missing their target as aiming at the wrong thing.

> Students aren't so much missing their target as aiming at the wrong thing.

This misdirection is relatively easy to address. Subtle adjustments of focus within our class practice can substantially change our students' perception of what is required of them when studying literature. The activities featured here do just this. They not only guide the students' first readings and initial analysis but provide a frame through which to view the rest of their English text studies.

UNPACKING A SENTENCE

Many comprehension and analysis activities in English textbooks presume that students are able to draw inference from a text. However, English teachers can't presume that students have learned this skill: we must explicitly teach it. A good way to embed this skill in a student's approach is to practise drawing inferences *one sentence at a time*.

This activity works best if you start with sentences with which the class is unfamiliar. Working with unfamiliar sentences seems to help students concentrate on closely examining the text for clues rather than basing their inquiries on their own prior knowledge.

Here are some examples that have been used to produce engaged discussions in senior English classes:

- In the afternoon, it was the habit of Miss Jane Marple to unfold her second newspaper. *(Agatha Christie)*
- Ted watched the orchestra through stupid tears. *(James Woods)*
- People's lives, in Jubilee as elsewhere, were dull, simple, amazing, and unfathomable—deep caves paved with kitchen linoleum. *(Alice Munro)*
- It was 1955 and we were driving from Florida to Utah, to get away from a man my mother was afraid of and to get rich on uranium. *(Tobias Wolf)*
- One day Karen DeCilla put a few observations together and realised her husband Frank was sleeping with a real estate woman in Boca. *(Elmore Leonard)*
- One night Miss Harper and Katherine are driving home from a celebration, a party at a hotel to which Miss Harper had been an unwilling guest. *(Elizabeth Jolley)*

This can take place as a warm-up activity at the start of a class and is easy to conduct:

1. Start the exercise by modelling this process on the board. Write up a single sentence and then annotate around it with the inferences you draw from this line. Underline and use arrows to make explicit from where you are drawing these inferences. Ask the class for their suggestions, always insisting they provide evidence to support their suggestions.

2. Put students in pairs. Provide them with another sentence. Ask them to conduct a 'think, pair, share activity' in which they brainstorm individually and then gather together all the inferences they draw from the sentence. Share these in a whole class discussion.

3. If they have not already done so, ask students to annotate the sentence as you modelled at the start of the exercise. Alternatively, get them to write a short paragraph summarising their analysis.

After this warm-up you can move on to a text you are currently studying. A lot of teachers who employ this technique start with analysing sentences and then move up to large blocks of meaning such as paragraphs or stanzas.

The final step of this process might then be to analyse a poem or a key passage from a text in this manner. One engaging way to do this analysis is to print the passage or poem at A4 size on A3 sheets so the students can draw links to the inferences they draw and to particular words or phrases.

Stanley Fish's *How to Write a Sentence* (2011) is both an excellent source of sample sentences and a fine resource for those wishing to explore this basic building block of literary study. Similarly, James Woods's book *How Fiction Works* (2018) employs close reading to analyse prose and poetry—particularly at the sentence level. It is a powerful model for this kind of nuanced analysis.

THREE-COLOUR HIGHLIGHTING

Students do not master material on a first reading. Nor do teachers. We need to recognise that literate readers are actually re-readers. In *The Literature Workshop,* Sheridan Blau argues that reading is a recursive process that in many ways parallels writing (Blau, 2003). After all, readers create drafts too.

The best English classes are ones in which students see the activities as an ongoing exploration of their own understanding: where they recognise that false starts, confusion and mistakes are part of the normal process of learning. In a great English class, students are shown that comprehension is not a product but a process (Beers, 2002). The *three-colour highlighting* activity is an example of this approach.

Instructions:

1. Have students do a 'cold reading' of a piece of literature such as a short prose passage or poem. Ask students to highlight any elements of the text that they find challenging, confusing or unclear.
2. Ask students to rate their understanding of the text with a mark out of ten. They may also wish to make some brief written notes about what they have read.
3. Ask students to discuss the reading with a partner. What did they understand? What did they find confusing?
4. Now have students read, highlight and rate their understanding of the text a second time. Make sure that they use a different colour highlighter or mark the text so that they can see how their level of understanding changes with re-reading and collaboration.
5. Ask students to discuss this second reading with another student or a small group of students. Alternatively, get students to share their thoughts in a whole group discussion.
6. Repeat the highlighting and ranking process a final time.
7. Ask students to reflect on how their understanding of the text changed over time. The simplest way to do this is by asking them to write a brief account of how their understandings shifted through three readings. Have them write down any questions they still have about the text.
8. Follow up with a whole group discussion to explore how the effect of multiple readings changed your students' views of the text.

Three-colour highlighting works because it acknowledges that first readings are tentative and partial: that something we don't understand in a piece of literature is not a barrier to knowledge but a jumping-off point. Being able to register how their level of understanding changes over time is a core skill of effective learners. This activity is unusually effective at fostering meta-cognition. It is one of my favourite activities for helping students 'notice what they notice'.

NOTE: Some teachers employ a code word task to introduce or reinforce this message about the conditional nature of our first encounters with text. See the Appendix on page 32 for an example of how to use code words in an English classroom.

REPLACEMENT TASKS

A common flaw of student text essays is that they simply retell the story: they paraphrase rather than analyse. Typically, this occurs because the student is not viewing the text as *constructed*. The student, of course, understands that the text has an author, but at some level they are not viewing the text as a product of a series of choices that the author has made—choices that can then be discussed and evaluated. Using a replacement task activity is an excellent way to encourage students to view a text as the product of the author's choices.

Replacement Activity One

Having students replace a series of words in the text is the most common form of this activity. The object of the exercise is for students to try and match the meaning, connotation and tone of the word they are replacing with their new selection. For example, you might ask students to do the following:

1. Identify the verbs in the first three stanzas of the poem. (You may not be able to presume that all students understand how to identify this part of speech. The *up and down game* on page 46 is a good example of a quick strategy you can use to help these students.)

2. Replace these words with verbs you have selected. Try as best as you can to make sure the replacement words have the same meaning and connotations as the original words. (As this is a poem and the sound of the words is also very important, you might also try to make sure your new words fit the rhythm of the poem.)

This is a challenging task and students quickly realise how hard it is to find a word that is as effective as that the author has chosen. Your follow-up discussion should explore this by not only asking the students for their replacement words but also discussing the choices they made to come up with their answers. Here are some sample questions commonly used to elicit these kinds of answers:

- Did you find this task hard?
- What is effective about the original word chosen by the poet?
- What other words did you consider instead of your final choice?
- Why did you reject these alternative choices?
- Of all the examples offered by your classmates is there one that better suits the rhythm of the poem or the style of the poet? Why?

Replacement Activity Two

Another classic replacement activity is to ask students in pairs to come up with replacement titles for the text. (This tends to work best for poems and short stories.) Asking for multiple titles actually makes this task easier as students feel less pressured when they don't have to come up with 'the one' alternative title that works. Setting the goal of multiple titles also helps them view the text from different perspectives (and ensures a jokey or impulsive answer is not the end of their thinking).

An alternative way of approaching a title replacement task is to give students a poem or very brief short story, having removed the title. Study the text as a class. Then ask students in pairs to come up with titles for the piece. Sylvia Plath's poem 'Mushrooms', for instance, works particularly well when used in this fashion. Tennyson's 'The Eagle' is another such example. This activity helps students tie together their various insights about the text and is one that they usually enjoy.

> This is a challenging task and students quickly realise how hard it is to find a word that is as effective as that the author has chosen.

THE CONNOTATIONS GAME

Replacement tasks are a good way to get students thinking about the connotations of words. Another way to introduce this concept is to play *the connotations game*.

Instructions:

1. Provide students with a list of synonyms for walking (strut, meander, shuffle, dawdle, amble, stride, saunter etc.).

2. Nominate a 'volunteer' and then ask this student to walk the length of the classroom. (This works best if the student is confident. Many teachers pick a 'look-at-me' student—that is, one who constantly seeks attention in class and for whom a task like this is a good chance to ensure that attention-seeking behaviour is used positively.) Now explain they are going to 'stroll' or 'dawdle' across the classroom. Ask for advice from their classmates. For example:

   - How is *strolling* different from *walking*?
   - Doesn't *stroll* just mean *walk*?
   - What are the other associations we have with *stroll*?

3. Have the students 'stroll' or 'dawdle' across the length of the room. Ask the students to give the person feedback on their efforts. Pick another word and repeat the process.

4. It is often effective to reverse the order of the process so that you select a word, and before the student moves they get advice from their classmates about how best to 'amble', 'wander' or 'pace'. This variation tends to be more supportive for the volunteer and works well with younger students or in classes where risk taking is limited.

5. Continue the process until the concept of connotation is clearly established with the group. ('Strut' is the most engaging example and is the perfect final word to help confirm the concept for students in a lighthearted way.)

6. An engaging follow-up that helps consolidate this learning is to have students now rank these synonyms according to speed of movement or clarity of intent (see the *support–challenge continuum* on page 73).

Taking Note

Too many good insights in English classes are erased by the bell. Too many important ideas discussed in a classroom never make it to the page. And in too many of the instances where information is recorded, it is done so in a perfunctory manner (a few illegibles lines in a notebook or an unfinished summary in a never-to-be-found again untitled file).

> Too many good insights in English classes are erased by the bell. Too many important ideas discussed in a classroom never make it to the page.

We must explicitly teach note-taking to students. They need easy-to-implement routines for précising key concepts and recording emblematic examples. Students need strategies for developing questions to shape their inquiries. They need frameworks for organising and mapping their developing ideas as these inquiries proceed. Most importantly, in an age of exponential growth in data collection, they need strategies for accessing, evaluating and using this information in a timely manner.

OPEN-BOOK INDEX CHALLENGE

Sometimes the most effective way to encourage students to improve their note-taking techniques is to get them to review their existing practice. The *open-book index challenge* is an engaging way for students to test the limitations of their note-taking strategies. It also leads to lots of group collaboration on how to refine these strategies in a way that encourages individual students to take ownership of this aspect of their studies. It is, in my experience, the only organisation activity that students routinely badger their teacher to do.

This activity has two components:

1. First, students review their own text, workbook or folders, listing either

    - all the skills or knowledge they have learned and numbering their workbook pages, or
    - key quotes, scenes, character developments, emblematic moments for discussion of themes etc.

    They then create an open-book index so they can quickly locate and retrieve this information. (Where students primarily use computers the principle is the same, but there is a greater emphasis on organising the folders on their desktop.)

2. Students then compete in a challenge activity to find out who in the class has the best-organised system of knowledge retrieval. To do this, the class completes the following steps

    - Set up the room so that two tables are facing each other side-on to the rest of the room. The teacher's desk will be at the front of the room positioned back from but between these two tables. The table should form a 'U' facing the rest of the class.
    - Nominate two students per table to sit at the front. They will be competing teams in the open-book challenge. Make sure each team member has their workbook, computer or text as well as their completed index in front of them.

- The challenge starts when you call out a key fact, topic or skill that the class has studied and the students race to find it in their workbooks. The first to find it receives a point. Teachers often let the groups compete for best of three. The winners of the challenge then stay at the table and two new challengers replace the losing team.

- While the teams are racing, the audience of remaining students also races those at the front. In this way they can still play an active role in the activity. The student whose book or set of files are organised so effectively that they beat their classmates then becomes one of the challengers.

The Open Book Challenge leads to lots of group collaboration on how to refine these strategies in a way that encourages individual students to take ownership of this aspect of their studies. It is also, in my experience, the only organisation activity that students routinely badger their teacher to do.

CUE SHEETS

Cue sheets are a classic replacement activity for the more traditional comprehension questions that teachers use to guide student note-taking.

A cue sheet is a list of carefully crafted sentence starters that have been designed to help students focus on the *process* of their reading. Instead of asking narrow questions about aspects of the text, they require students to note the development of their own perceptions as they read. This moves students beyond recall to analysis and interpretation. Cue sheets remind students to move beyond 'what?' in their note-taking to 'why?' and 'how?' and provide a structure that is open-ended enough to support student reflection without producing generic, narrow or formulaic responses.

Cue sheets not only help students flesh out their thinking about a *specific* text but also give them a set of strategic questions that they can use whenever they approach any text. They cue students to employ the kinds of cognitive strategies that produce high-order responses and to explicitly learn the kind of approaches 'that come as second nature to successful readers and writers' (Peterson, 2002).

> Cue sheets not only help students flesh out their thinking about a specific text but also give them a set of strategic questions that they can use whenever they approach any text.

Teachers will have their own sense of what kinds of questions will help their own students, but if you are looking for a model, the following list (closely adapted from Carol Booth Olsen's 'Cognitive Strategies Sentence Starters' from her 2011 book, *The reading/writing connection*) is an excellent starting point.

CUE SHEET FOR GUIDED READING

Closely adapted from Carol Booth Olsen's 'Cognitive Strategies Sentence Starters' (2011)

Planning
The learning intention is …
The purpose of this activity is …
My goal here is to …

Forming Interpretations
What I think is going on is …
I think this means …
I'm getting the idea that …

Tapping Prior Knowledge
This connects with …
I already know that …
This is kind of like …

Monitoring
What I should concentrate on next is …
This confused me because …
I need to re-read the part where …
I think I'm on the right track because …

Asking Questions
Do you think …
What if …
How does …

Clarifying
The part that still confuses me is …
I think this is right but I need to …
Perhaps I should go back over …
I need to research …

Predicting
I think …
Probably what might happen is …
If _____, then …

Revising Meaning
I used to think _____ but now I think …
I've changed my mind on that because …
My latest thought on this is …

Visualising
If this were a movie …
I can see …
In my mind I can picture …

Reflecting and Relating
One key idea then is …
So a conclusion for me is …
This is important to me because …

Making Connections
This makes me think of …
This is similar to my own life in that …
I can understand this because …

Analysing the Author's Craft
The line that catches my attention is …
I like how the author _____ to show …
A phrase/word that stands out is …

Summarising
The key idea here is …
Basically, what's happening is …
A quick way of saying this is …

Evaluating
It would work better if …
I don't like this because …
What the author values is …
I think the most important idea is …
I like this because …

Adopting an Alignment
I connect with this character because …
I really got into this story when …
I identify with this author because …

SPLIT-PAGE ANALYSIS

Split-page analysis is a reading and note-taking strategy in which students use a folded sheet of paper to identify and then interrogate key ideas in a passage of writing. The activity is a very simple two-step process that produces complex thinking about texts:

- In the left-hand column of the folded sheet, the student summarises the main concept from each paragraph.
- In the right-hand column they list any questions they may have about these ideas.

Interrogating each point encourages students to view their work as a dialogue between what the text is saying and their own response to these ideas. S L Meyer, who developed this activity, originally labelled it a 'folded paper dialogue' (cited in Young, 2008).

> Students are more likely to produce a response that is in their own voice, as opposed to a stilted one that awkwardly regurgitates what others have said about the text.

A real strength of this approach is that students are more likely to produce a response that is in their own voice, as opposed to a stilted one that awkwardly regurgitates what others have said about the text. This is especially the case when students are exploring critical material as the dialogue structure helps students to maintain a critical distance between the author's positions and their own views.

IDENTIFY IDEAS:	**EXPLORE IDEAS:**
Summarise key points of each stanza or paragraph	*Ask questions about each key point*

Paragraph One:
Right from the start the author tells us that a rich man will be on the look out for someone to marry.

Questions:
Did everyone really think this? Is this true now too? And how much do they mean by 'good fortune'?

Paragraph Two:
All the people of the area are so sure that this is true that they think that the man is almost owned by their daughter who wants to be the person they marry.

Questions:
Is it the man who really thinks this or the families in the neighbourhood? Why are they so obsessed with marrying off their daughters? Is Austen sort of being sarcastic? Or ironic?

Paragraph Three:
His wife has found out gossip about who has rented that place and wants to tell him about it.

Questions:
Why does she call him Mr Bennet instead of his name? Aren't they very close? Why doesn't he just say yes he would? Doesn't he really want to hear about it? Did everyone speak like that then?

Paragraph Four:
A rich guy from the north has rented the place and is sending his servants down to get it ready.

Questions:
What is a chaise and four? Who is Mr Morris? When is Michaelmas?

Paragraph Five*:
The man's name is Bingley and Mrs Bennet (the wife) wants him to marry one of her girls. She wants her husband to go and arrange this but he doesn't see the point.

Questions:
Why can't she go and speak to Bingley? Why does he joke about his wife marrying Bingley? Is he trying to compliment her to get out of going?

*Actually several short paragraphs of dialogue.

NOTE: Despite the simplicity of this structure, some students who are unaccustomed to this form of note-taking will struggle with this activity, and it is crucial that you provide sufficient modelling when introducing a split-page analysis.

SEE, THINK AND WONDER

Over the last thirty years, English students have been expected to study not only written texts but also images, film and, increasingly, online texts. Obviously, many of the techniques used to help students examine printed material can be applied to visual information, but there are some strategies designed specifically for this type of text.

Probably the most well-known exercise for examining visual images, the see, think and wonder technique was first developed by Project Zero at Harvard Graduate School of Education. It is a simple device that asks students to frame their response to visual material by responding to three simple questions:

1. What do you see?
2. What do you think about that?
3. What does it make you wonder?

There are lots of ways this can be used in classes, but probably the best known of these exercises is the film still version of this task. First, select some key images from a film you are about to study. (Obviously this also works with other multimodal texts, such as the homepage of a website.) Then present this series of images to the class (pausing the film on this image is the simplest way to do this) and have students answer each of the See, Think and Wonder questions as a group. Alternatively, students can record their responses in a brief three-part statement: 'I see … I think … and I wonder … '

> Students are encouraged to learn the habit of centring their discussion on closely observed visual detail and then drawing inferences from these observations.

Exploring the mis-en-scène of a shot or the layout of a website in this way heightens the student's attention to visual detail. It also models the pattern of analysis you want them to bring to their written work on film and multimodal texts. Students are encouraged to learn the habit of centring their discussion on closely observed visual detail and then drawing inferences from these observations. As with the best analytical text essay responses, though, it doesn't end at inference but instead asks students to speculate about the wider implications of their thinking or the limits of their understanding.

By breaking a student's response into separate categories, this simple tool has a number of profound effects on their learning:

- It requires them to demarcate between what they see and the presumptions they draw about this impression in what are often visceral first responses.
- It reminds students to look in a more sustained way at what it is exactly that they are seeing before jumping to further conclusions.
- It encourages students to value simple observation as an important skill in itself (which is especially important for students who might be reluctant to take part in class discussion because they find drawing inferences difficult). This builds confidence and often leads them into taking a more active part in discussion activities.
- It deepens their inquiry beyond these impressions to focus on the implications of their thinking, encouraging them to frame their response to the material around further inquiry.

SILENT SCREEN/BLANK SCREEN

This is another simple but effective set of exercises for exploring a film text. Simply select a scene from early in the film that is emblematic of the filmmaker's technique in either sound design or cinematography and direction. Now play the scene to students, but either turn the sound down so they see only visual information or play only the audio from the film. Using the class discussion techniques mentioned earlier in this chapter, unpack what the students have noted when focusing exclusively on one sensory element of the text.

This exercise is effective for two main reasons:

- It heightens student awareness of *constructed* elements in film that students see as naturally occurring. For example, musical cues on the soundtrack or key lighting of a character.
- It concentrates on a smaller set of features for the student to study. Multimodal texts like film have a very high number of constituent parts, and targeting attention in this way helps students avoid being swamped in complex information when first approaching a text.

Conducting Classroom Discussions

Fast and Effective Assessment (Pearsall, 2018) explores in detail the subtleties of running a classroom discussion. This craft is important for a teacher of any discipline but particularly for English teachers, as the class discussion is probably the most essential tool English teachers have for exploring texts and sharing insights. Classroom conversations shape the complexity of a student's thinking about texts and set the expectations of the depth and detail of their responses. Indeed, much of the modelling that shapes a student's written approach to a text is actually verbal. Many teachers find, for instance, that refining their questioning technique improves their students' use of quotation or the degree of sensitivity they bring to an unsympathetic character. Better questions mean better answers.

> Much of the modelling that shapes a student's written approach to a text is actually verbal … better questions mean better answers.

However, one of the significant challenges of improving the quality of the class discussion is that the techniques involved are often naturalised to such an extent that expert teachers aren't consciously aware when they are employing them. They are just running a 'normal' class discussion. By naming these techniques we can identify the constituent parts of highly effective practice and emulate what great English teachers do automatically.

On the following pages are the top ten questioning techniques for exploring a text in a whole group discussion. (For a more extended exploration of these techniques see *Fast and Effective Assessment*.)

THE TOP TEN STRATEGIC QUESTIONING TOOLKIT

1. **Cold Calling:** Sometimes referred to as the 'No hands up rule', cold calling is asking students a question without waiting for them to indicate whether or not they have the answer. English class discussions are often dominated by a handful of able and articulate students, and this can undermine the value of the discussion to the rest of the group. Cold calling ensures that a whole-class discussion genuinely involves the whole class.

   It is important that even the form of the question reflects this aim. Cold calling works best if instead of naming a student and then asking a question:

   'Michael, why does the protagonist do this?'

   You actually ask the question so all students consider the issue you are raising, and then, after a pause, identify a student:

   'Why does the protagonist do this? ... Michael?'

2. **Question Relay:** A technique used to ensure students don't answer cold-called questions in an unthinking fashion. When a student wants to shrug off a question with a knee-jerk 'I don't know', you ask them to listen to two other responses and determine which is the best response.

   'OK Li, you are not sure why the character does this ... I'm going to ask two other people, and then I'm going to ask you which of those answers you prefer.'

3. **Wait Time/Pause Time:** Wait time is the time between when you ask a question and when you expect an answer. The average wait time in an English discussion is very low, less than two seconds. This does not give students enough thinking time to formulate their views about complex issues and often results in the fastest-thinking students dominating class discussion. Just being mindful of how you use wait time can have a profound impact on the number and quality of responses. For instance, waiting three to five seconds can triple the number of student responses.

   Lengthening pause time can have similarly positive effects. Pause time is the amount of time you pause after a student answers to give them an opportunity to add greater detail to their response or to self-correct. Extending pause time makes it more likely that students will include examples in their answers and encourages students to review their first impressions. Routine use of pause time is a characteristic of English teachers who are accomplished at facilitating class discussions.

4. **No Glossing Rule:** One of the crucial measures of highly effective teaching is 'the depth of student processing of knowledge' (Hattie, 2009). That is: do the students do the thinking work in your English classes or do you? In class discussion, teachers sometimes do this by 'glossing'. Instead of waiting for a complete student answer, you accept a partial response and then fill in the rest of the answer yourself. Having a no glossing rule helps you to identify this common trap and avoid it.

5. **Rich Questions:** Accomplished English teachers ask open-ended questions that elicit detailed and sustained responses. Of course, these teachers also ask closed questions, typically to build a scaffold towards more complex thinking. However, what is significant is that they organise their inquiries around the rich high-order questions:

    'What drives the protagonist to do this?'
    'How does the form of the poem shape its meaning?'
    'How has the author elicited sympathy for this character?'

6. **Inverted Questions:** Inverted questions are a way to come up with rich, open-ended questions very quickly. To do this you simply invert the question so that the answer to a closed question is actually included in the question stem itself:

    Closed Question: *'What is the character's name?'*
    Answer: *'Mr Thomas Gradgrind.'*

    Inverted Question: *'The character is called Thomas Gradgrind. Why does Dickens call him that?'*

7. **The Golden Question:** The questions we ask in class discussion should elicit the kind of answers we also want in written work. For instance, if we expect students to support observations in their essays with detailed examples from the text, we must seek the same kind of evidence with our questioning. The simple follow-up question 'What makes you say that?' is an effective way to elicit this 'evidentiary reasoning' (Project Zero, n.d.). The routine use of simple question formulations like this ensures students are in the habit of justifying their answers with detailed textual evidence.

8. **Elaboration Cues:** English teachers are constantly reminding students about the importance of depth and detail in their work.

Elaboration cues are a set of techniques teachers employ in class discussion to guide students towards these more detailed and thoughtful answers. These techniques include placeholder statements, reflective statements and blank prompts.

Placeholder Statements

Placeholder statements are short, neutral phrases that teachers use to ensure that they are not passing immediate judgment on a student answer. In his *Assessment and Learning Pocketbook* (2007), Ian Smith calls these statements 'minimal encouragers'. He offers the following as effective examples:

'Go on ... '
'Mmm ... '
'Oh?'
'Then?'
'And?'
'I see ... '
'Really ... '

Reflective Statements

Alternatively, you might use reflective listening to indicate that you understand a student's response but still leave them room to qualify or add detail to their answer. This is simply a matter of restating the student's response indicating your understanding of *their* viewpoint:

'So you are arguing that ... '
'It seems that you feel ... '
'So what you are saying is ... '
'You think we should view this as ... '

Blank Prompts

Another good technique for encouraging student responses is to frame your responses as though you were unsure of an answer. This signals to students that they are chiefly responsible for developing a response to the question. This is largely communicated through tone, but some teachers go as far as actually suggesting an incorrect or simplistic answer in the form of a question:

'So what comes after a topic sentence again?'
'So the poet's only use of form is rhyme? Is that right?'

9. **Second Draft:** In the most sophisticated class discussions, students carefully listen and respond not only to teacher questions but also to each other. Second drafting is a technique for encouraging this kind of interaction. When a student gives an answer that is correct but perhaps lacks clarity or detail, you ask other students to rephrase the answer in more specific, precise or formal terms.

   Teacher: *'If you find yourself paraphrasing instead of analysing, what technique have we practised to change this? ... Ravi?'*

   Ravi: *'Do that first sentence thing where you talk about ideas?'*

   Teacher: *'Can someone come up with a second draft of that answers using more formal language? ... Amanda?'*

   Amanda: *'Make sure your topic sentence is about an idea rather than an event.'*

10. **Exampling:** Another way to encourage students to carefully listen and respond to each other is to ask them to provide examples to support each other's suggestions. This is particularly effective because it allows you to check whether students understand a question in only the narrowest sense or whether they are able to draw a larger inference from their classmates' insights.

    Lucinda: *'She wants to marry off her daughters because they need a man to economically support them in such a patriarchal society.'*

    Teacher: *'Can you find another example to back up this idea of the limited options available to women in a male-dominated society? ... Darren?'*

    Darren: *'Charlotte marrying Mr Collins.'*

Distant Reading

Close reading is a core skill for studying literature. Examining an author's use of form down to the sentence level, unpacking the connotations of a particular word choice, and exploring the way a specific scene employs imagery are all skills that students need to build up a plausible and well-supported investigation of a piece of literature.

However, students also need to recognise broader patterns in texts or groups of texts. Understanding genre, investigating the context of a text's production, and identifying views and values in an author's work or era are skills that provide broader understanding of literary texts. (We deal with this in greater detail in the next chapter.) Most literary study is a constant back-and-forth dialogue between a close examination of individual passages of writing and these wider concerns.

> Distant reading programs reveal new insights about texts that simply would have been impossible before the advent of these technologies.

One new method for introducing these concerns is through 'distant reading'. This type of textual analysis uses digital tools to see underlying patterns in very large amounts of information. Google's Ngram Viewer, for instance, searches an enormous database of published works to show word usage over time. Word cloud programs show word frequency across an entire novel or even all of an author's oeuvre. Distant reading programs reveal new insights about texts that simply would have been impossible before the advent of these technologies. Their use is growing exponentially, and it is worth considering whether students in your class might benefit from occasionally employing these highly engaging programs when exploring texts.

WORD CLOUDS

Word clouds are a type of program that has become widely used right across the curriculum. However, word cloud programs are particularly useful in the English classroom where they can be used for pre-reading and reflection exercises. The following steps show how to create a word cloud and use it as the basis for a learning discussion in an English classroom.

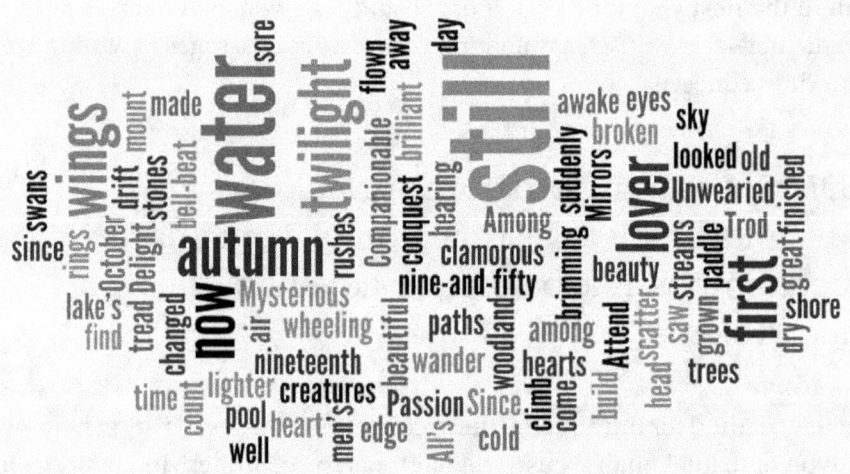

Instructions:

1. Create a word cloud for a text, poem or student work. This involves simply copying the selected document and pasting it into the text field of a word cloud-generating website. Tagxedo and Wordart are popular examples that have easy-to-follow prompts. Cloudart and Wordsalad (School's Edition) are similarly useful apps for Mac users. The program will count all the words in the document and then represent the frequency of these words in a cloud like the one on page 28. The larger the word in the cloud, the more frequently it appears in the selected text.

2. Provide the class with copies of the word cloud. It tends to work best if students work in groups of three or four.

3. Explain to the class how this image has been created. Ask the class to carefully study the image and predict what the text will be about. It is important that teachers allow students the time to consider other ways to view the word cloud—we have to help students move beyond first impressions.

4. Have students unpack their predictions in a whole-class discussion. Don't ask for 'the answer': instead, encourage students to discuss how they approached the word cloud and what evidence they studied to come up with their ideas. Effective questions might include:

    - What did you look at first?
    - Did you group any words together?
    - Are there any other words that you could add to the groups these students have suggested?
    - Can anyone piece these groups of words together into an overall story?
    - Is there anyone who can predict what this word cloud is about?
    - Are there any words that don't seem to fit with this reading of the word cloud?
    - How does this word fit then?

5. Now get students to read the passage in its original form and then continue your class analysis. An obvious jumping-off point for this discussion is the differences between the students' predictions and their first reading of the text itself. Students will usually start discussing this comparison with their partners without prompting, so once they

have read the text proper this can provide a fairly seamless transition into a class discussion about the features of the text.

There are three main ways English teachers employ word cloud activities.

Poetry/Passage Word Clouds

Create a word cloud of a passage or poem and then get students to predict what is happening in the text upon which the word cloud is based.

This approach makes students highly alert to connotation and emphasises the importance of seeking out and grouping evidence. When the class moves on to exploring the text in its original form, it also gives you a chance to highlight how form shapes meaning. These are all skills particularly suited to close reading of a passage or poem.

Exemplar Word Clouds

Provide students with word clouds of exemplar answers and then use them to identify the language features of excellent responses.

Asking students to compare the exemplar word cloud with a word cloud of their own response is a good way to do this. The insights that students receive may be obvious (stronger responses are more analytical, referring less to characters and plot events and more to the author and their ideas – often using a wider range of synonyms for these ideas), but the real strength of this activity is that students discover these insights for themselves.

Secondary Text Summaries

Using word clouds to provide a summary of the key themes or ideas in critical material or ancillary reading about the primary text.

Word clouds can offer students a simple key-word synthesis of the core information in a supplementary text. A word cloud of a piece of critical material, for instance, can give students a quick introduction to the position and tone of the author. A pre-reading activity like a word cloud can also give your students an opportunity to discuss the sometimes alienating, challenging or unfamiliar language of literary criticism.

Again, a teacher could simply explain the author's position and tone, or provide a definition of key terms in a worksheet, but in discovering it for themselves, students are practising some key features of literary analysis and doing it in an engaging fashion.

NGRAM VIEWER

The Ngram Viewer (https://books.google.com/ngrams/info) employs Google's repository of digitised texts to allow the user to graph word usage over time. Google's data set is enormous, currently representing five hundred billion words published in eight languages over the last five hundred years.

The Ngram Viewer is intuitively designed and easy to use. You simply enter words or phrases into the search field and nominate the period of time over which you would like to search. A comma must separate each item. The program then produces a graph comparing the frequency with which these terms appeared in published material over the set period.

Obviously, there is not a *direct* correlation between word use and the prominence of an idea within a specific time period, but getting students to speculate on possible explanations for each Ngram is a good way to introduce a theme, issue or time period featured in a text. Below is a short list of examples of searches that have been productive in senior English classes (if the search was used in a class as part of a unit on a specific text, the novel or set of poems is listed in brackets).

- Contrast the use of 'lady', 'woman' and 'wife' between 1700 and 2000.
- Trace the frequency with which the artist Chagall is mentioned in German language between 1920 and 1950 *(Night)*.
- Explore the changing use of the word 'God' since 1600 *(Songs of Experience)*.
- Track the frequency with which the word 'slave' appears in English from 1800 to 1900 *(Beloved, The Adventures of Huckleberry Finn)*.
- Compare the popularity of 'democracy' to 'monarchy' since 1750.
- Contrast the changing prominence of the terms 'wedding' and 'inheritance' in English texts between 1770 and 1820 *(Pride and Prejudice)*.

An excellent way to introduce the Ngram Viewer to students is to get them to use their own name and that of their friends or siblings. (This is an especially effective strategy for students who might be tempted to trial inappropriate terms.)

Appendix: Code Words

A code word task is an engaging activity for rehearsing text-study skills. A short, sharp exercise that is challenging but not impossible, it is a classic example of deliberative practice. Typically, this task involves giving students coded material that contains information about a text you are about to study. Students decode this information in small groups and then go on to use the same skills to 'decode' a challenging literary text. The 14th century Scottish ballad 'The Twa Corbies', with its use of archaic terms and mysterious narrative, is a perfect example of the type of text that can benefit from this approach.

Instructions:

1. Select or create the key information you want students to closely scrutinise. Address it to the students, and sign off as you would a letter.

2. Highlight the chosen text. Open the drop-down font menu in the formatting toolbar. Select one of the 'nonsense' fonts, such as Webdings or Wingdings, and change the font. It is best to double-space your text and use a large font of 18 point or above. As a guide, one page of code text takes students approximately fifteen minutes to decode.

3. Divide students into groups of four to six. Hand out the code word sheet. Explain to students that they have to decode a message about your chosen topic and that there is no key to the code, but they need to keep in mind three important clues:

    - The text the students are decoding is a letter and follows the conventions of that form.
    - It is addressed to them from their teacher.
    - It contains no punctuation and some words start on one line and finish on another.

4. Give students eight to fifteen to complete this task. Closely monitor student progress but avoid intervening straight away if a particular group is struggling.

5. As the groups finish, take the time to check their code's accuracy and acknowledge their achievement. Make sure that they write out the decoded statement in their books. Finally, instruct them to synthesise the material into a short statement written in their own words.

An effective way to do this is to get them to write the statement in exactly twenty-one words.

Not all teachers will see the relevance of this activity for an English lesson: as a stand-alone activity it is engaging but teaches no specific text-study skills. However, when twinned with a follow-up 'decoding' activity it can become a powerful way to get students to think about the incremental nature of how we read texts. A warm-up code-breaking activity helps activate the mindset that is required to investigate challenging texts. Having had to decode words that they don't understand and infer meaning from context clues, students are often quicker to recognise that they can read a challenging text even if they don't understand every word or phrase.

Chapter 2
WORKING FASTER, READING DEEPER

Practising Skills and Deepening Inquiry

One of the challenges of teaching literature is that we must ensure our students have a comprehensive knowledge of the set text while also helping them develop the skills to analyse this information in a complex, high-order way. This is a delicate balancing act. Just exploring the foundation knowledge of a text can be incredibly time-consuming: lessons about the basic details of plot, character and setting will expand to fill whatever time is devoted to them. This knowledge development is important but the lesson time devoted to it must be carefully proportioned. After all, students must also explore the thematic concerns of the author, investigate how the text is constructed and research how others have responded to the text while developing their own view of it. So how do you ensure your students do all this when some are struggling just to know what happened in the book?

There is a two-part strategy that is very effective for finding this balance. Firstly, teachers must employ activities that condense the amount of teaching time spent on the foundation study aspects of literature. This doesn't mean they avoid teaching students about plot, setting and character—there is no substitute for students knowing a text well—rather, teachers need to have a bank of strategies for accelerating this knowledge acquisition. They need short, sharp, formative activities that help students develop a detailed knowledge of the text in an efficient manner.

Secondly, teachers must employ techniques that encourage students to explore texts in a sustained, high-order fashion. The study of literature requires students to move beyond their first impressions and see patterns and connections. It requires students to consider the complex motivations of characters and to think long and hard about how and why a text was created. Teachers need a bank of activities for encouraging students to deepen their inquiries. They need text-study strategies that challenge habitual thinking and foster reflection.

This chapter offers teachers a range of effective techniques for employing this two-part strategy in the everyday English classroom.

Foundation Knowledge

Just getting through the book can swamp all other activities in an English class. There are a variety of reasons for this. Students, for instance, tend to use all the class time allotted for studying the basic features of a text without necessarily using all that time effectively. However, it is a trap to think that this is just an issue of student application. It is also one of course design. Foundation inquiries can colonise the time devoted to a text and teachers must carefully plan their foundation study to ensure it is effective, yet allows enough time to also teach higher-order critical reading skills.

> Just getting through the book can swamp all other activities in an English class. It is a trap to think that this is just an issue of student application.

The seven activities in this chapter are examples of the kind of exercises that allow you to do this. These versatile activities can be carefully seeded throughout your everyday curriculum. Quick but highly effective, they remind teacher and student alike that foundation studies are merely the starting point for our study of literary texts. After all, the test of effectiveness when working through a text is not content coverage but our depth of understanding.

SEQUENCE STRIPS

The activity that best embodies the two-part approach of revising foundation knowledge while deepening student inquiry is the sequence strip activity.

Sequence

1. Explain to students that you are going to review the plot or narrative structure of the text (or a section of it) that you have just learned.
2. Ask students, in pairs, to list the twelve most important events or scenes from the text.
3. Have students rip their page into thin strips with one event per strip. Mix the strips until they are out of order. (This activity also works well if students write out each event as a bubble in a mind-mapping program on their notebooks.) Ask them to swap their strips with another and then put the strips back in sequence.
4. Review the pairs' suggestions and ordering of events in a whole-class discussion. Actively correct misconceptions that are not peer corrected.
5. Ask each pair to combine with another and repeat the process. Alternatively, they might combine with another pair to form a group of four to review the sequences again. This can be repeated with a group of eight or even as a whole class.
6. Ask students to create their own lists of the text's events. They can base their work on the suggestions of classmates but can add events that they think have been overlooked. This need not be limited to twelve events.

Rank Order

7. Now ask your students to put the strips into 'rank order': that is, from most to least important event in the text, of those that are listed. For younger or less able students you will need to define what important means, but for older students, coming to an agreement about how to define importance is a useful and productive part of the discussion.
8. Repeat steps two to five. As a final reflection activity, ask students to submit an individual list ranking key events. It will need to be accompanied by a short, written justification as to why those scenes or events are so important to the text.

INSTANT PICTURE BOOK

An *instant picture book* is a similar narrative summary activity but it also has the advantage of working with poetry. Underpinning it is the idea that when students apply knowledge in another context (such as using images to summarise written information), they are more likely to remember and understand that information. The great advantage of this task is that it is more engaging and effective than a comparable comprehension task, but it can be done much more quickly. (Indeed, it is important that the picture books are done instantly as some students need a clear signal that this is not a test of their artistic abilities.) The example below focuses on poetry but this activity works just as well with key scenes from a novel, play or film.

Instructions:
1. As a class, conduct a group analysis of a selected poem.
2. Then, in pairs, ask students to select eight quotes from the poem that reflect its narrative arc. Explain to the class that they are looking for lines, phrases or even single words that when grouped together tell the story of the poem.
3. Instruct each pair of students to make an eight-page booklet by folding two sheets of paper in half.
4. The pairs assign one quote to each page of the booklet. Then they come up with a quick illustration to match these quotes.
5. As a reflection task, conduct a gallery session for students to display and discuss the resulting instant picture books. (Sometimes teachers will also ask their students to write a brief reflective commentary to justify their selections and explain their illustrations.)

This simple exercise often produces quite sophisticated results. Students find that telling a story in 'borrowed lines' allows them to demonstrate their understandings of the text—even if they don't yet have the language to do this in their own words. They quickly get a sense of the narrative's arc. Drawing the pictures gives them an opportunity to then synthesise this knowledge in a conceptually challenging way. The instant picture books they produce make good revision aids during further study.

Borrowed Pictures

A variation of this activity is to ask students to not only borrow the words of the poems but the images to go with them. There are a number of online resources that make doing this much easier than having to bring to class stacks of magazines or newspapers (though this approach can be very effective ... and messy).

To try this variation with your class, simply follow steps 1 to 4 (above) and then have students illustrate their quotes using a photo repository or storyboarding website. Sites such as 'Bubblr' on Pim Pam Pum or storybird are two well-known examples of this type of resource but there are new ones going online all the time. This is a less intimidating task for those who are worried about their drawing skills, and the high-quality production values of the final product often makes for a particularly memorable revision aid.

If you are searching for resources for introducing an instant picture book activity, Matt Madden's *99 Ways to Tell a Story* (2005) provides a model for the myriad different ways you can tell a visual story. *Literature for Life* (Cahill & Pearsall, 2005) has a range of student examples.

RACE THE BELL

This activity has many names and is also known as *beat the buzzer, race the clock* and *countdown*. While there are many different variations, the basic concept is always the same. Students formulate a question that they can ask each other about the text. They then stand as a class (students who can't stand indicate they are 'up' in a fashion they nominate.) A volunteer then asks a question of the whole group. Using hands up, the teacher identifies a volunteer to answer. If they are correct, both the person who answered the question and the one who asked it, get to sit down. The aim of the game is that everyone will be seated by the time the bell goes.

This is a great knowledge-review activity and can be used by English teachers in a host of different ways. One of the most productive areas to use this activity is in helping students revise their knowledge of a text's minor characters. Students often overlook the significant role secondary characters play in a novel, film or play. (Experienced teachers are familiar with the analytical essay in which it seems as though only the protagonist and their love interest appear in the text at all.) Setting the text's minor characters as the topic of a game of *race the bell* is a good way to start addressing this issue. Just formulating questions for their classmates gets students thinking about the role minor characters play in the text. The actual activity then provides a chance to review this knowledge in an engaging way.

SYNTHESIS TASKS

Synthesising plot information is one of the most effective activities for helping students remember the events of a play, novel or film. Indeed, synthesis can be used for all sorts of activities that help students master the foundation elements of a piece of literature.

Synthesis is a high-order skill. It requires students to make complex decisions about what in a text is important and what is not, and then present this information in a concise fashion. Students benefit from being given scaffolded ways to practise this skill. Two popular examples of this approach from my work with teachers are the *exacto* and *cheat sheet scramble*.

> Synthesis is a high-order skill. It requires students to make complex decisions about what in a text is important and what is not, and then present this information in a concise fashion.

Exacto

Summarising information with acute brevity is a neat way to encourage students to think deeply about what the core elements of a text are. In an Exacto, students are required to summarise the events of a passage, chapter, scene or entire text in a precise number of words. Typically, this will be a very low number. Plot summaries of just thirteen or twenty-one words work particularly well; setting a very low word limit seems to make the exercise into a fun challenge for students. (If a student is struggling you can double the word limit. They will find the task much easier but still produce a concise synthesis.) The finished plot summaries can then be used as the basis for other exercises such as the *plot box* task on page 72.

Cheat Sheet Scramble

A cheat sheet scramble is another fast, formative activity with which to explore foundation elements of a text. A cheat sheet is a piece of blank A4 paper (A3 for younger students) that has been folded over twice so that it is a quarter of its former size. Students are then asked to synthesise all their learning on a particular topic on just two sides of this folded sheet (effectively half of one side of an A4 sheet). In a scramble, students display these cheat sheets in a gallery session and then carefully review each other's efforts.

Instructions:

1. Ask the students to open up their folded cheat sheets so that both sides of the summary are visible. Have them display these sheets on tables positioned centrally in the room.
2. Tell students you are going to conduct a gallery session where the students review each of the sheets and nominate which of the summaries they find most helpful.
3. Once they have selected their favourite cheat sheet in the scramble, they then identify it using stickers or labelled tokens. (Good labels include 'This helps me', 'This successfully meets all criteria' or 'Can I have a photocopy of this as a model?')
4. Once the class has identified particularly helpful model answers (typically three or four sheets will get the most votes), ask class members why they voted for a particular sheet.
5. You might also ask the students who created the most popular sheets about the decisions they made in creating these cheat sheets.

NOTE: It is important to appreciate that some students may feel exposed during this process. To protect these students, a cheat sheet scramble completed in small groups of four or five might be more appropriate.

TESTING FOUNDATION KNOWLEDGE

Formative tests are a powerful way to focus a student's attention on mastering foundation knowledge about a text. They serve as a clear hurdle, nudging students beyond approximated understandings where they have a general sense of narrative, character and plot but are unclear about specific details.

Traditional tests are quite common. Many teachers favour the surprise quiz to test if students have read the homework chapter or understand who all the characters are. However there are a range of other types of formative test that are also effective in an English class.

Student-Composed Revision Test

Students have to write a test that could be used as a revision exercise for testing their classmates' knowledge of the text. Typically, this contains five true or false questions, ten multiple-choice questions and five short-answer questions. Student must also submit an answer sheet. A good follow-up activity is to create a final revision test composed of individual questions collated from the students' tests.

Open and Closed Quiz

This is a two-part exercise. First, students complete a quiz under test conditions. Then, changing their pen or font colour, they revise their answers under open-book test conditions, referring to their notes or to the text itself. This will help students identify what they know, both with and without assistance. It will also signal to you what they don't know that they don't know.

Confidence Test

Instead of completing a test, students simply review each question, providing a mark out of ten to indicate how confident they are of answering it correctly. A standard follow-up is to then actually get students to complete the test and rate their finished answers to see if their confidence ratings were accurate. This quick and effective exercise works particularly well if you have limited class time for reflection or are exploring a longer text with lots of narrative information.

70/30 Exam

Students are provided with a test that has been completed by their teacher, who has deliberately answered 30 per cent of the test incorrectly. Students are then expected to correct the test and identify the mistakes.

FOUR TELL

This activity is a good way to quickly recap the events of a text and is typically used as a quick precursor to other text-study activities. It is a simple and easy to organise strategy.

Instructions:

1. Select four able students who know the text well. Explain to them that they will each have to retell the story of the text to their classmates. They will only have two minutes to do this. Send the students out of the class to give them a chance to plan what they want to say. Emphasise that this time is for individual planning and they must not confer while they are out there.
2. While these students prepare their two-minute narrative summary, discuss with the rest of the class your expectations about their role as an audience. This not only means listening respectfully but also being alert to the differences and similarities between the accounts. Students also need to pay close attention to omissions. Direct them to listen for what is left out of each account.
3. Ask the students to come back into the room one at a time and give their two-minute plot summary. After the first two summaries, conduct a class discussion comparing and contrasting them. After they are all finished repeat this discussion.
4. As a quick reflection activity, get students to write a dot-point plan of what they would include if they had to speak in front of the class (or what they would change if they had to do so again).

Four tell is a great lead-in activity—it takes only ten to fifteen minutes to complete and is both engaging and effective. It works well because students get to hear multiple versions of the same information and they are hearing it not from a teacher but their own classmates. Four tell is particularly helpful for those who have a limited knowledge of the book because it gives them a scaffold through which to understand further discussions of the text. It also provides an extension opportunity for students who have already mastered this text.

One of the most popular ways to follow up four tell is to do some small-group essay writing exercises. The four speakers, as well as those who have contributed most to the class discussion, become leaders for each group, ensuring that every group will have a good base of text knowledge on which to draw.

THE UP AND DOWN GAME

This is another fast, formative activity for revising narrative information. In the *up and down game*, the teacher makes a statement about the text and students indicate whether the statement is true or false by respectively standing up or sitting down. This simple activity works particularly well if students come up with the statements themselves—writing one true and one false statement about the text on a strip of paper that the teacher then reads to the class.

There are several variations and important techniques for getting the most out of this activity:

- Students are demonstrating their knowledge in a very public forum so you must include 'layers of protection' for students who might feel exposed by this activity. Teachers should, for instance, offer other signal options for students who find movement difficult (thumbs up or down works well). Similarly, scaffolding such as a cheat or study sheet or the opportunity to use an open-book index will provide less able learners with a handy support mechanism.

- If you are running this for the first time it is important to plan your statements beforehand as it is sometimes hard to come up with false statements on the spot. Indeed, it is always worth having a list as it is surprising how many questions you get through in this energetic and easy-to-play game.

- You can have a fast and furious five-minute activity where students are reminded of a previous day's learning, but there are also more considered versions of this activity that work well as a plenary task. A longer, more speculative version of the up and down game where all students are asked to justify their answer can be very revealing—students are much more likely to explain their process if they have to justify an answer that they don't yet know is true or false.

Reading Deeper

Literary texts are sophisticated constructions and a good deal of the pleasure in studying them lies in understanding their complexity. We want our students to understand and respond to these more challenging aspects of a text. However, we cannot presume that our students can automatically do this. It is our responsibility to guide their study. The key is encouraging students not to settle for their first impressions—they need to challenge their presumptions and test their ideas. We must encourage our students to:

- consider how the ideas and events in the text might link with their own lives
- map out relationships between ideas, events and characters within the text
- record their thinking about a text as it develops
- test the plausibility of their insights.

Above all, we must encourage our students to *suspend closure* and think beyond reductive logic and received wisdom. Second thought class activities such as *reading process reports*, *line debates* and *prompt generators* offer practical techniques for achieving this goal.

> The key is encouraging students not to settle for their first impressions—they need to challenge their presumptions and test their ideas.

READING PROCESS REPORTS

There are many different ways for students to record their interactions with a text: comprehension book notes, weekly practice essays, journals, reading logs and chatroom posts. In most cases, the expectation is that students tell us what they *thought* about the text. However, there is great merit in also hearing what a student is *thinking*.

Reading process reports are an attempt to get students to record the tentative development of their understandings of a text. The key difference from other types of reports is that students not only essay their views about a text but also explicitly map how they came to these views. A reading process report might include comments about how a student's view changed over time, careful noting of what is confusing or difficult, discussion about approaches successful or otherwise as well as digressive thoughts and associations the text evokes. It is an attempt to get students to show their working out. Reading process reports are designed to foster metacognition. Validating speculative, partial and provisional readings, these reports encourage students to notice what they notice.

> In most cases, the expectation is that students tell us what they *thought* about the text. However, there is great merit in also hearing what a student is *thinking*.

Reading process reports are a departure from other types of literature writing tasks, and it is worth thinking carefully about how they are best introduced to a class:

- Teachers usually start this task by asking students to complete a cold reading of a short poem or brief passage of prose. However, selecting a passage from a text that students have studied but is less familiar to them also works well.
- One strategy for doing a cold reading is to conduct a three-colour highlighting activity (see page 8–9). Instead of asking students to just rate their understanding of the text out of ten as they normally do in this activity, ask them to also record dot-point notes about what they have discovered and what they still find confusing. These notes can

then be used as the basis for writing a process report that maps the development of their understanding as they first encounter the text.

- Another strategy is to employ screencast tools that allow students to record their real-time impressions of a text. Screenpal is an easy to use example (as is Screencast-o-matic), but there are innumerable screencast applications that could be used here. Simply send students a soft copy of the chosen passage or poem, and have them record themselves talking their way through first and subsequent readings of the text. Focus questions for this task might include
    - What do you first notice here?
    - What is confusing or difficult?
    - What approaches are you taking to clarify your understanding of the text?
    - What else does this text make you think of?
    - How has your understanding changed in the course of this reading?

    The advantage of screencast tools such as Screenpal and Screencast-o-matic is that students can do this on their own without having to negotiate the social or logistical complications of working with a peer. (For instance, taking dictation effectively requires a threshold of literacy skill that a student might not have, and young people can sometimes see thinking out loud as embarrassing.)

- Alternatively, some educators such as Jeffrey Wilhelm (2001) advocate using a thinking-aloud protocol where students work in pairs to record each other's first insights by dictating them to a partner. This can be done in person or in an online forum. This acts as a powerful signal to the group that everyone develops their point of view over time and helps students see explicitly that they build their answers through the back-and-forth of working with others.

Once students have built up some notes on the reading process, they can then write them in a formal report. This works best when students are explicitly asked to not only answer the dot-point questions listed above, but also reflect on what this process has taught them. When students write up their reading process report, you can prompt them to include some kind of reflection on themselves as a reader, the challenges of reading this particular text and discussion about the reading process in general (Blau, 2003).

PROMPT GENERATOR

Teachers often use essay prompts as a way of guiding their students' investigations of a text. One of the limitations of this approach is that the prompts can seem arbitrary. Students can feel that the ideas they are asked to explore bear little connection to their understanding of the text or indeed to their lives. Answering essay questions might be something they do in English, but for them the relevance of the task ends at the classroom door.

Giving students a chance to compose their own questions is a powerful way to address this concern. One such technique is Gretchen Bernabei's *prompt generator*. This technique provides students with a scaffolded way to create their own essay prompts and thereby 'tie personal meaning to the literature they have read' (Bernabei, 2005).

Instructions:

1. Ask students to identify a minimum of five key ideas or themes that the class has identified while exploring the novel. Alternatively, you may wish to present students with a list of themes.
2. Instruct the class to put these themes into the left-hand column of the prompt generator grid (page 51).
3. Then ask them to identify one positive thing about the first of the themes. The statement should be a general one about the theme rather than the book. Bernabei labels this a 'truism'.
4. Now have students identify one negative aspect of this theme.
5. Ask the class to repeat the process, filling in the grid with positive and negative statements for each of the themes on the list.
6. Discuss the students' responses as a whole class. (You may wish to create a list of prompts for each theme.) Explore how effective these prompts might be as a topic for an essay about your set text. You might ask students to identify the statement to which they have the strongest personal response, or check whether these statements might be combined into more effective prompts.
7. Ask students to write an essay employing one of the prompts they or their classmates have created.

GRID FOR *PRIDE AND PREJUDICE*

THEME	POSITIVE	NEGATIVE
Love	'Love requires looking beyond your first impressions.'	'Love can lead you into being deceived.'
Family	'Families can provide support and understanding during difficult circumstances.'	'Families can limit your choices or opportunities as an individual.'
Pride	'Pride in your achievements creates confidence to take on new challenges.'	'Pride can lead you to overestimating your abilities or underestimating others.'
Ambition	'Ambition drives you to reach your full potential.'	'Ambition can create manipulative or mercenary behaviour.'

LINE DEBATING

A line debate is a popular activity for exploring issues within a text in a dynamic way. It teaches students to justify their answers and encourages them to see contested views of a text from both sides. The activity is commonly used as a precursor to essay writing; however, it can be used to tease out the nuances of any key question readers might have about a text.

Line debates inject playful competition and kinesthetic activity to the literature classroom. They allow teachers to frame discussion around contrasting ideas—a powerful way to raise student engagement and understanding (Wiliam, 2011). Most of all, they demonstrate the collective power of the class group for working together to 'unpack' issues in a text. To conduct a line debate:

1. Introduce the topic the students will be debating. (Many teachers use an essay prompt.)

2. Divide the class into an affirmative and negative team, and have them stand on either side of the room. Explain that they need to come up with arguments to support their assigned side of the debate irrespective of their personal views on the topic.

3. Outline the rules of the debate
    - Members of each team take it in turns to volunteer their arguments. (One common variation here is to require the student or a teammate to offer a supporting quotation to justify their side's argument.)
    - If the debater is able to offer a new argument to support their side they can select one of the opposition team to join their team. (If a class member changes sides three times, they are 'locked' and can't change sides again. This avoids the stronger debaters being ping-ponged back and forth across the room.)

4. Conduct the debate. It is crucial that you have a means of noting down all the points that are made. This might mean recording the debate or assigning students to act as scribes.

Continuums

A powerful way to conclude a line debate is to mark out a continuum from strongly agree to strongly disagree with the debate prompt and ask students to line up in the position that reflects their personal view. This *belief continuum* is an instructive activity in its own right. Continuums allow students to position themselves not just as for or against a topic but in degrees of intensity about that view. Those with no strong view either way can position themselves in the middle of the room. You can then hold a discussion in which students justify why they are standing where they are. The power of this activity is underlined by the fact that students, without prompting, often reposition themselves when someone offers a persuasive justification for their own position.

Continuums can be used to tease out many other aspects of our response to a literary text such as:

- common characteristics of a genre, where students line up from 'always present' to 'never present'
- the emblematic aspects of a poet's oeuvre, from 'representative' of their wider work through to 'non-representative'
- characters, by judging from 'sympathetic' to 'unsympathetic'.

Four Corners

Sometimes, however, you require students to explore concepts that don't easily fit on a simple continuum. If you want your class to explore a more multifaceted issue, you can conduct a *four corners* activity. In this activity, you assign a student to each corner of the room, and group the rest of the class in the centre of the room. Each 'corner advocate' then argues why his or her viewpoint is correct. The rest of the class votes with their feet as to which 'corner advocate' has the most persuasive argument and can join in the debate from the corner they align themselves with. This works well with a question such as 'Who is the most important/sympathetic/interesting character?', but is especially effective when comparing different (critical) readings of the text. Again, it is the discussion here that helps test the validity of particular positions, thus deepening student understanding.

Kinesthetic activities like line debating and the other continuum games bring the body back into learning. This is important in a potentially sedentary subject like English. It stimulates memory, and in linking physical movement with specific knowledge creates a mental image of that knowledge that serves as a powerful non-linguistic representation of student learning (Dean et al., 2012; Jensen, 2001).

Developing Understanding

Literature introduces its readers to other voices and other lives. It encourages us to grant to others the complexity of our own motivations. Literature is an act of sustained empathy that demands the same from its readers.

How do we encourage our students to take a sensitive and sympathetic approach to all the characters they encounter in texts? It is not easy. Sometimes it is hard for someone still finding their own voice to be open to those of others. Young people can find it difficult to understand characters and situations that are radically different from their own perspective.

> Literature is an act of sustained empathy that demands the same from its readers.

In this section we explore some strategies that can guide students towards this goal:

- Character ranking activities help students see how characters can reveal the underlying views and values of a text.
- The hidden thoughts activity encourages students to move beyond their first impressions and consider the motivations of unfamiliar or unsympathetic characters.
- Role-play activities place students in the position of the character themselves, asking them to consider their inner lives.
- Critical material auctions encourage students to explore other readers' views of the texts and its characters and to evaluate their plausibility.

These exercises provide a framework for exploring character in a considered and empathetic fashion. They are powerful teaching tools for the everyday English class.

CHARACTER RANKING

Character ranking is an excellent strategy for exploring issues of views and values in a text. This exercise offers teachers a simple means to prompt students to discuss complex questions: How does the author position readers to respond to the text's characters? Does this change as the work progresses? What would have been the common attitudes towards the characters in the society in which the text was produced? Or the society in which it was set? Do we now, as readers, view these characters differently?

Instructions:

1. Have students list the characters in your text. (Teachers often ask students to do this alphabetically or in the order in which they appear in the text.) Alternatively, teachers may give students a set of laminated cards with a character's name on each card.

2. Ask the students to reorganise this list of characters according to whether or not the author endorses the character's values. Students can list them on a continuum from the character whose values the author most strongly supports to those whose values he or she condemns.

3. Have students justify their rankings to a partner or the wider class. Once they have clarified their thoughts through a discussion, ask them to justify their view in a short written piece.

There are many variations of this activity. You can also ask your students to rank and re-rank the characters according to the following criteria:

- whether or not the society or community in which the text is set endorses your characters' values (You might then compare this with how we view the characters in our context.)

- who are the most likeable or sympathetic characters

- how the author's positioning of the characters changes over the course of the text (This is done by asking the students to compare and contrast one of the rankings mentioned above at both the start and the end of the text.)

- whether or not our view of the characters has changed over the course of rereading the text. (Have students complete an initial reading ranking and then a subsequent reading ranking on any of the above criteria.)

Each of these criteria can produce a complex discussion about character and the underlying views and values of a text in a quick and effective way.

HIDDEN THOUGHTS

In this activity, students are required to answer a sequence of rich questions that lead them to better understand other people's perspectives. The hidden thoughts strategy has many applications in an English classroom, but it is particularly useful for helping students understand the motivations of characters.

Sometimes students find it hard to empathise with or even understand certain characters in a text. This distant or dismissive approach can substantially undermine their analysis of a text. Characters that tend to be misunderstood or overlooked in this way include those from another era or of a different gender than the student, those acting according to religious duty or honour, or characters from within a framework of extremely limited choice or life experience. The hidden thoughts protocol (Cahill, 2008) is an excellent way to address this issue.

> Sometimes students find it hard to empathise with or even understand certain characters in a text.

Instructions:

1. Ask students to draw a stick figure at the bottom of a page. Alternatively, students can use storyboarding programs or comic book apps to draw their diagrams (Comic Life and Comic Book are popular examples). The height of the figure should be no more than an eighth of the page. Instruct them to name the figure for the character they are meant to represent. Explain to your class that they are going to be exploring the 'hidden thoughts' of this person.

2. Have students draw a thought bubble above the head of this figure.

3. Explain to the class that you are about to give them a series of prompts to explore what this character might be thinking. For each question they are to write the answer in a separate speech bubble. They need to draw the bubbles so that they have space for six to ten bubbles to fit on their page.

4. Ask students to answer each of the questions below. Make sure you leave appropriate time for reflection between each response, and pause occasionally to get students to share their answers with the class.

   - What is this character thinking?
   - And what else are they thinking?
   - What is this character feeling?
   - And what else?
   - What do they hope for?
   - And what else?
   - What do they fear?
   - And what else?

   NOTE: Sometimes teachers ask their students to answer the first question again at this point to underline the way their thinking has changed.

5. Prompt students to share and compare their answers through a class discussion or gallery session.

6. Finally, have them apply their new insights about the character in a short analysis, character profile or essay.

This simple but elegant piece of pedagogy is very effective for cueing students to deepen their thinking about the motivations of others and understand the issues characters face in a more complex way.

ROLE-PLAY ACTIVITIES

Role-play activities help students explore literature in a more empathetic fashion. Students can try on perspectives other than their own without social risk. Acting as 'key informants', they can evaluate commonly held perspectives from the point of view of the characters or actual stakeholders. Role-play activities offer students the confidence and protection of a role while investigating a text.

> Role-play activities offer students the confidence and protection of a role while investigating a text.

Hot Seat

In a hot seat discussion, a group of students play characters from a text, and their classmates interview them to better understand the characters' motivations and perspectives. There are lots of variations of this activity, but the basic version is easy to set up and makes for a compelling class activity:

1. Select the students who will play the main characters of your text in the hot seat discussion. (Some teachers also include the author of the text or prominent critics who represent a particular reading of the text.) Explain to these students their role, emphasising the importance of preparation and research. Give them sufficient time (at least a couple of days) to complete this preparation.

2. Explain to the class that it will be their job to interview the classmates who will be playing these main characters. They will need to prepare at least one question for each character.

3. Once they have created this initial list, they select two of these queries as 'questions on notice'. Explain that these will be submitted to students playing the characters ahead of time to improve the sophistication and quality of their answers. Many teachers set up an online forum for students to post these questions. The advantage of this approach is that it allows the 'characters' a way to access the questions outside of class. For the students asking the questions, it provides a series of models to use when formulating their own questions. The forum also serves as a public accountability guarantee, 'nudging' students doing the questioning into seeing their role in the exercise as an active one.

4. Prepare the classroom for this discussion. Most teachers set up a half-circle of chairs facing the class. However, some teachers who have more experience or are more confident in the activity use the fishbowl design: they set the characters up in the middle of the room facing each other and arrange the rest of the class around them. The great advantage of this design is that it encourages the characters to respond not only to the audience but also to each other.

5. Conduct the hot seat discussion with the teacher (or a class leader) acting as moderator. Organise the questions so all characters get an opportunity to speak regularly throughout the debate. Encourage follow-up questions and cold call on students to elicit further queries and more sustained discussion. Give the characters a chance to ask each other questions. Usually this discussion is recorded by scribes or on video.

6. Debrief with the class. Then ask students to write a reflective piece, essaying their reactions to the activity. (For younger students, a popular form for doing this is a news report.) Make sure they address a key question: did their view of the characters and how they are depicted change or develop over the course of the discussion?

Literature Trial

A literature trial is an extended hot seat activity. Using the format of a legal hearing, it encourages students to consider contested issues within a text. Its great appeal for teachers is that the adversarial form of the trial fosters a particularly rigorous approach to evidence as students prosecute or defend their case. Students tend to emerge from this activity with a greater appreciation of precise, close readings that support their thesis.

To conduct a trial:

1. Identify a contested issue in the set text. The guilt or innocence of a particular character works well, but the issue need not be a legal crime. Any debate about a character's actions that is at the heart of the text will produce powerful results. This issue should then be framed in clear adversarial terms, much as you would compose a debating topic:

    - Mr Bennet is guilty of neglecting his daughters.
    - Friar Lawrence is responsible for Romeo and Juliet's deaths.
    - Medea should be executed for her crimes.
    - Harry Potter should be expelled for trespass.

2. Explain to the class that they will be conducting a trial hearing to determine the answer to this issue. Assign trial roles to the students. You may wish to use a volunteer survey to do this, asking students to nominate three roles they could play in order of preference. Alternatively, you can simply assign the roles yourself to match your students' strengths. A good selection of roles would include: judge (can be played by teacher), prosecution team of at least three, defence team of at least three, witnesses for prosecution and defence, the accused character, a jury and a court reporter. Key roles will need understudies to cover for absences and workload concerns.

3. Outline the basic rules and procedures of a criminal hearing. Legal studies texts written for a high school audience are an excellent source of succinct information on the topic. However, you'll often be surprised by how much students have picked up about trial procedure just through depictions in the media.

4. Typically, the students write a reflection statement on what they learned from the trial exercise. Sometimes this is supplemented or even replaced by a creative response in which students write about the exercise from the perspective of a trial participant or observer.

The great strength of a literature trial is that the process is strongly student led.

The great strength of this exercise is that the process is strongly student led (though you should be mindful of casting roles carefully and avoiding 'tricky' legal strategies). Many students who have completed the task reflect on their growing confidence with the text. It is also a powerful way to model a group approach to the text to instil in the class a sense of collective efficacy.

CRITICAL MATERIAL AUCTION

Reading another person's view of a text can add to the depth and detail of our own responses. However, students must be careful about the material they select. Rote answers cribbed from text guides or the internet are the antithesis of the thoughtful, personal responses we are training our students to produce. We must explicitly teach our students to evaluate critical material with a discerning eye. The critical material auction is an engaging way to do this.

Instructions:

1. Put students in groups. Explain that each group will be completing an analytical essay on your current text. To aid this, each group will be asked to select a range of reference materials. Their job will be to evaluate the relevance and usefulness of this critical material.

2. Explain that each group will be given a research grant of $2000 in auction money with which to purchase the critical material they deem to be most useful for them. This material will be auctioned. Once students have bought their preferred critical material, they will work together to create a written response using only the resources they have purchased at the auction.

3. Distribute materials and give groups an opportunity to review each item. They will need substantial time to do this effectively. Ask each group to rank these resources in order of how helpful they would be in completing the written task.

4. Remind students that they can only use the resources they purchase in the auction. (Students will routinely 'sneak' quotes from material they do not intend to buy into their notebooks. Tacitly encourage this process by turning a blind eye to this kind of important note-taking.)

5. Auction the critical materials with yourself or a class leader taking the role of the auctioneer. (One engaging way to lead up to the bidding is to have a series of essential information that students must buy at fixed prices.)

6. After finishing the written task, ask students to reflect on the usefulness of the reference material they selected. Was it as helpful as they anticipated?

This is a great activity that works just as well for printed and online materials. The challenges presented by this task are typically about classroom management, rather than a need to prompt students about good research practices. Having only one nominated bidder and 'fining' those who call out or are too loud are effective strategies for maintaining a calm but engaged atmosphere.

NON-LINGUISTIC REPRESENTATIONS

Information is stored in the brain in the form of words and images (Paivio, 2006). English classes explore linguistic information, so sometimes there is a tendency to overlook the value of non-linguistic representations of knowledge. This is a mistake. Using non-linguistic representations of knowledge is one of the most powerful tools for increasing student achievement (Dean et al., 2012). It helps students process and remember information, organise the knowledge into a conceptual framework and link that knowledge to other learning. This is especially helpful when exploring complex works of literature.

Here are a couple of examples of how you might employ non-linguistic representation in a literature class.

Sociograms

A sociogram is a graphic representation of the social links between groups of people. It is a particularly effective tool for exploring the relationships between characters in a text. Indeed Johnson and Louis (1987) have described constructing a sociogram as 'a most valuable' literary activity for classroom teachers in English.

In its simplest form, a sociogram lists all of the characters of a text and their relationship to each other. Each character is represented by a circle that is labelled with their name. The characters' relationships are then depicted by arrows and the relative positioning of the circles to each other.

It is in drafting and redrafting the design of the sociogram that students deepen their understanding of the text. The best sociograms demonstrate the complexity of the characters' interactions in novel ways, but there are some simple conventions that help students create sound sociograms:

- Central characters are placed at the centre of the diagram.
- Major characters are given larger circles than supporting characters.
- Close relationships are suggested by close spacing; characters more distanced from each other are separated on the page.
- Relationships are mapped with lines connecting the character circles and arrowheads, colour coding and labelling are used to designate the nature of the relationship. (A line between two characters labelled with a love heart and each way arrowheads would depict a romantic relationship whereas the same label with only one arrowhead might represent unrequited love.)

- Broken lines represent problematic relationships; thicker lines represent stronger connections between the characters.
- Key descriptive words are often included in the character circles to help summarise the text. Short quotes can also be used to describe characters, their interactions with others or justify the design of the sociogram.

Drafting is an important aspect of this process. Students can use paper or mind-mapping software to try out multiple options before settling on a final design. My current favourite site tool for making sociograms is Creately, but this is an area where designers have provided teachers with a rich array of options.

> English classes explore linguistic information, so sometimes there is a tendency to overlook the value of non-linguistic representations of knowledge.

Asking students to explain their design choices to the class or a classmate is an excellent way to conclude this task as it asks students to justify their reasoning. Getting students to work in pairs is a good way to ensure that, even if you don't have time for this follow-up activity, justification and discussion will be a core part of this task as students have to collaborate on their sociogram design.

Venn Diagrams

Teaching students strategies for identifying similarities and differences has a powerful positive influence on their learning (Dean et al., 2012). A Venn diagram is a graphic organiser that helps students draw these kinds of contrasts. Venn diagrams consist of two or more overlapping circles that students can use to compare and contrast ideas. Each circle represents a distinctive aspect of the text such as theme, character, narrative style or point in the plot. Where the circles overlap, students list information common to both categories. This simple process can produce complex investigations and discussions in a literature class.

Chapter 3

GETTING IT IN WRITING

Text Analyses & Essay Responses

Teaching students to put their insights about texts into writing—or develop them through writing—is one of the most challenging aspects of teaching English. Essays and other types of written text responses are complex constructions that involve a student organising their diverse thoughts about a piece of literature into a coherent and fluent piece of writing. How do we teach this subtle and nuanced skill? How do we get students to move beyond narrow, pro-forma essay structures or the 'paraphrase-heavy' derivative answer?

In this chapter, I will explore the constituent components of analytical text responses and offer activities that teach students that excellence is something that can be made. It can be incredibly empowering for a student to realise that sophisticated essay responses are actually built up from a series of simple techniques. This emphasis on an ongoing strategic approach encourages persistence and builds academic resilience (Dweck, 2006). When students can see that complexity comes not from some personal ability ('I could never do that') but from a rhetorical strategy or other technique ('That's *how* you do it'), they are more likely to work harder and for longer to improve their writing.

> It can be incredibly empowering for a student to realise that sophisticated essay responses are actually built up from a series of simple techniques.

The challenge, then, is creating deliberative practice exercises aimed at developing these simple skills: exercises in which students can isolate a particular technique, rehearse the activity in a structured way that allows them to make lots of mistakes and then get fast and effective feedback on their performance. Accomplished English teachers don't just identify the weaknesses in their students' essay responses but have a suite of strategies to specifically address those concerns.

The activities featured here offer practical techniques for 'nudging' students out of the bad habits that commonly lead to poor writing. They teach the rhetorical strategies that are the building blocks of fluent and sophisticated essay responses. They provide effective ways to challenge able students and support those who are struggling. And for teachers of literature, they offer engaging and simple learning strategies that are as compelling as our subject matter.

Refining Essay Technique

Essay writing requires more than just a fluent prose style. There is a range of subtle skills that students must master to compose a successful analytical text response. Typically, skills such as selecting textual evidence or organising ideas into paragraphs are practised as part of an integrated approach to essay writing. Similarly, précising narrative information and writing effective introductions are often rehearsed as students write entire practise responses.

However, it is also important to use deliberative practice activities where students can work on these skills in isolation. Teachers and students can then hone each specific skill through focused feedback and repetition. This type of targeted exercise can be much more engaging than the 'massed practice' of writing many practise essays, and research suggests it is also more effective for building enduring mastery (Brown et al., 2014).

> Essay writing requires more than just a fluent prose style for a successful analytical text response. There is a range of subtle skills that students must master.

The seven activities provided here are rigorous and engaging examples of this kind of deliberative practice.

BUNDLING SWAP

Probably one of the most difficult challenges in teaching essay writing is teaching students how to structure their responses. Many student essays demonstrate some knowledge and insight about a text but present this point of view in a convoluted or confusing fashion. The obvious response from many teachers is to give students a generic structure to follow, but this often replaces one common problem with another—the stilted, formulaic response.

Using an essay writing formula like TEEL can be very helpful for some students, but there is a danger that by concentrating on the formula students are moving away from the text itself. Sometimes students don't need to practise putting their ideas into a formulaic structure – so much as they need to practice finding structure in their ideas. They need practice grouping their diverse thoughts. Bundling is an effective way to practise this specific skill.

In a bundling exercise, students write out all their ideas on strips of paper or, using mind-mapping software, onto their computers. They then group these thoughts into 'bundles' of related ideas, these bundles becoming the essay's paragraphs.

Instructions:

1. Divide the class into small groups (groups of four seem to work best). Ask the group to brainstorm a list of 'first thoughts' in response to an essay question or a passage of writing. Have them use the think, pair, share protocol to ensure each student comes up with individual ideas of their own before creating a group list. Students record these ideas on strips of paper.

2. Instruct each group to swap the strips with another group. Tell the class it will now be each group's job to collect these ideas into four or five bundles, with each bundle representing a set of related ideas.

3. Explore the approach of each group in a class discussion.

4. Repeat the process so groups get lots of deliberative practice at bundling ideas. Do this for as many iterations as time permits, but organise it so that, finally, students must do their own set of idea strips.

5. As a final exercise ask the class to individually write up an essay plan based on their group's bundling of their own ideas. This task can be extended into a skeleton essay or even a full essay response or passage analysis.

This is a useful exercise for teaching students to structure their responses without lapsing into formula.

QUOTATION STRIPS

In this variation of the sequence strip activity, students are asked to rank how useful a series of quotes are for responding to a specific essay prompt. It is a great way for students to practise seeking out evidence to support a contention. This activity is a good example of deliberative practice. Students can rehearse responding to a range of essay prompts in a short space of time while getting fast, formative feedback on their skill at using quotations.

Instructions:

1. Ask the class to list ten emblematic quotes from your text and write each of them on a strip of paper. Alternatively, you can provide students with a set of laminated quotes from the text or list them on a worksheet (see page 71).

2. Write an essay prompt on the whiteboard.

3. Ask the students to rank the strips according to how useful each of their quotes might be in responding to this prompt. Many teachers have students do this in pairs or small groups so students can tease out their own thinking by having to justify it to their classmates.

4. After discussing how the different quotes were ranked as a class, repeat the process with a different prompt but the same quotes. This change of essay topic is crucial for training students to get used to addressing a wide range of prompts about a single text. (In the course of an average lesson, a student can repeat this process for up to ten different essay prompts—the equivalent of planning ten practise essay responses.)

Getting students to nominate which other quotes they might employ if they had to respond in essay form to a particular essay prompt is an effective way to extend this activity.

One commonly used reflection activity for this exercise is having students write a skeleton essay for one of the prompts they were given. This works best if the skeleton essay contains a full introduction (or contention) and the topic sentences and quotations for each key paragraph of the student's essay plan.

QUOTATION STRIPS: WORKSHEET

Which of the following quotes would be most useful if you had to answer one of these essay prompts? Rank each quote from one to eight in the column provided for the first prompt. Now repeat the process for the second prompt. Did the rank order change significantly between the different prompts? What other quotes might you add to this selection to answer either of these prompts?

- 'Macbeth is entirely responsible for his fate.' Do you agree?
- 'This dead butcher and his fiend-like queen.' Is this a valid assessment to make of Macbeth and Lady Macbeth?

MACBETH QUOTES	PROMPT 1	PROMPT 2
'of this dead butcher and his fiend-like queen' *Malcolm*		
'It is a tale/ Told by an idiot, full of sound and fury, Signifying nothing.' *Macbeth*		
'unsex me here,/ And fill me … full Of direst cruelty.' *Lady Macbeth*		
'Yet I do fear thy nature It is too full of the milk of human kindness To catch the nearest way' *Lady Macbeth*		
'… for none of woman born shall harm Macbeth' *Apparitions*		
'Methought I heard a voice cry, "Sleep no more! Macbeth does murder sleep"' *Macbeth*		
'If it were done, when 'tis done, then 'twere well It were done quickly' *Macbeth*		

THE PLOT BOX

There is a widespread tendency for weaker writers to paraphrase a text rather than analyse it. Elsewhere in this resource, we look at ways to shape *reading* practices so that this is less likely to occur in student *writing*. What approach should teachers take if this has not worked? One effective strategy is simply imposing a limit on the amount of plot information students can use in their essay responses. This strategy is effective not because students always manage to fit within this limit but because trying to do so makes them more conscious of their use of paraphrase. In this sense, the *plot box* exercise is a useful example of deliberative practice: it doesn't tell students about the value of analysis, it shows them.

Instructions:

1. Ask students to write a forty-one word summary of the narrative events of a text. You may vary the number of words involved according to age and ability, but students should attempt to come up with precisely the number of words you have nominated.

2. Before students write their next essay response, ask them to retrieve this summary piece. They then affix it to their draft sheet or place it at the top of a Word document in a text box.

3. Explain that the only plot description they can mention in their essay must appear in this plot box. Students may change what is in the box but cannot add extra information beyond the word limit.

Feedback Box

An interesting variation of this activity is to get students to use a reminder box like this for teacher feedback. When they are handed back a corrected essay, ask them to summarise your feedback in their own words. As is the case with the plot box activity, setting an arbitrary word limit can make this an engaging précis activity. The next time students are writing a response have them affix this feedback summary to their work as a reminder of the improvements they are trying to make in their work.

SUPPORT–CHALLENGE CONTINUUM

Can your students discuss with subtlety an author's stance on issues explored within a text? Many English teachers find that while their students understand an author's viewpoint, they tend to express that understanding in absolute terms. Similarly, students will sometimes miss the nuances of an author's position (ironic or unreliable narrators are a particular problem), and their essay will present a simplistic analysis of the views and values of the author:

'Jane Austen hates Mr Collins.'
'Carey is showing us that Herbert Badgery is just a liar.'

This problem seems to be exacerbated when the analysis being expressed is not the student's. It is both harder to understand and express the subtleties of a position when it is the 'borrowed viewpoint' of a teacher or study guide.

This exercise is designed to get students thinking about the degree of intensity with which an author holds a position. It also helps students select appropriate synonyms for expressing their analysis.

Instructions:

1. Present students with a range of words they can employ to describe an author's viewpoint on a particular element of the text. Your list will range from those that indicate a strong endorsement of a particular view through to absolute condemnation. The list below is a representative sample:

Value	*Damn*	*Sanction*	*Support*	*Question*
Endorse	*Challenge*	*Undermine*	*Attack*	*Dismiss*

2. Have students order these terms along the length of a *support–challenge continuum*. Do this first in small groups and then as a whole class.

3. Ask the students to now use five of the terms in sentences about the author's viewpoint on issues explored within a text.

   'Twain condemns the institution of slavery and what it does to an individual like Jim.'

   'Finally, we see that the playwright sympathises with those who act with humility before the Gods.'

In senior classes, these sentences can be integrated into a cohesive paragraph exploring the author's views and values.

INVERSE MODELS

In *Classroom Dynamics,* I explore the value of using inverted models when a teacher is finding it hard to change a student's practice:

> Sometimes when students don't seem to be picking up on a particular piece of feedback and are making the same mistake over and over, you can get them to see the mistake for what it is by asking them to deliberately create an answer full of these mistakes. By creating the 'worst response in the world' students are positioned to take a more distanced view of their work and see patterns of poor practice. (Pearsall 2012)

The inverted model technique is particularly useful when teaching students how to write a high-quality essay introduction. (In fact, I first developed this technique when students in one of my classes continued to produce very poor introductions despite being taught repeatedly the traps to avoid.)

Instructions:

1. Explain to students that they are going to try to write the worst introduction in the world (WIITW). It will be their job to write an introduction that employs common faults of essay introductions. Students will need to be reminded here that while they are being asked to deliberately produce a poor model answer, all other class conventions still stand: the work will employ correct spelling and grammar and won't be offensive or inappropriate.

2. Ask students to list the features of poor introductions. As a starting point you might provide some examples via board notes:
   - passive voice
   - plot summary over analysis
   - themes presented as a laundry list.

   Getting them to look back over their notes about writing successful introductions is also helpful. However, providing actual samples of poor essay introductions is usually the most engaging and effective technique.

3. Now get students to create their WIITW using the list of poor features as a reference point. When they are finished have them annotate their example.

4. Finally, get students to write an introduction that avoids all of these common traps. You might get them to do this by rewriting one of the poor samples you provided.

NOTE: This activity only works when the task is discrete, takes a short amount of time and leads directly into another version of the exercise proper. Some teachers provide students with a worksheet to ensure the exercise is treated seriously and is framed as deliberative practice. The risks associated with this task are worth taking because the answers make great inverse models and encourage students to take risks and avoid repeating common mistakes.

What To Avoid Essay Sheets

However, if you feel this type of exercise would be confusing for your group or lead to silly responses, you might wish to try a different form of inverted model exercise. A *what to avoid essay sheet* works well. Simply create an inverted model of whatever response you are seeking students to create and then ask students to annotate these features.

> **Inverse Model Essay Introduction:**
>
> Hamlet was a play written by Shakespeare in 1608. Its themes are death, revenge and tragedy. The play is about a prince whose father is killed and then how his son pretends to be mad while plotting his revenge, but after accidentally killing his (the King of Denmark's) advisor the play ends in tragedy with lots of characters dying. These three passages are different scenes from the play that show imagery, alliteration and the author's point-of-view.

Attached to an exercise sheet or assessment task, this will make students more aware of which traps to avoid and reduce the amount of your correction directed towards avoidable error.

These are great fun to work up as an English team. They help us think about not just individual student errors, but the patterns of error within our classes and ways to discuss addressing these errors.

EDITING YAHTZEE

Editing Yahtzee is an activity designed to give students a chance to review the terminology your class employs when discussing essay writing practice and by extension to use this meta-language to improve the editing of their own writing. It works particularly well if timed so that the exercise is completed before an assessment task but after students have produced a sample answer.

Instructions:

1. Assemble a collection of essays that can be used as examples for this activity. The previous year's assessment responses work well. Where possible, collect a higher number of examples than you have students in the class. Alternatively, take a handful of carefully selected responses and make multiple copies of each. Label or number each individual essay.

2. Make up a Yahtzee sheet that features the structural and analytical strategies you wish students to include (or avoid) in their essays. Examples might include:
   - topic sentence
   - grouped evidence
   - thesis statement
   - woven quote conclusion.

3. Put the responses in a central pile and explain to students that they must find an example for each of the elements listed on the Yahtzee sheet from these essays. The key rule is that they must find only one example per essay.

4. When students have completed their Yahtzee sheet repeat the exercise with their own sample responses. Having practised identifying these strategies (or traps to avoid), they should be able to not only make changes to their response but also label and categorise the changes.

5. A challenging and engaging variation of this activity is to use critical material instead of student essays. A number of schools currently use this activity as an extension task with able groups or reserve it for use late in term four.

SIXTEENS

Throughout this resource we have discussed the enduring tendency of weaker student essays to concentrate on the character's experiences within the text rather than examining those of the reader and how the author shapes this experience. Asking students to practise turning observations about the character's world into observations about the author's construction of these elements is a simple technique for addressing this persistent issue.

Instructions:

1. Ask students to list sixteen statements about the text. Teachers sometimes provide this list to students or give the class an essay topic to focus this process, asking them to complete the task in groups using their collective notes.

2. Instruct the class to rewrite these statements to address how the author has constructed meaning or to describe the reader's experience in the text. Have students highlight the statements that already meet this criterion. Students will often have more observations about characters and events, and some will complain that it should have been made explicit that they needed to produce observations about the text's author and readers. Make it clear that the purpose of this exercise is to practise turning these observations into ones that address authorship and the experience of readers.

3. Model this conversion process with the class.

    Gatsby is obsessed with Daisy.
    Fitzgerald explores Gatsby's obsession with Daisy.

    Elizabeth doesn't like Darcy at the start of the novel.
    The reader is positioned to share Elizabeth's initial dislike of Darcy.

    Some teachers use this modelling as an opportunity to explicitly revise with students what is the subject of a sentence, exploring the difference between passive and active sentences.

4. Complete this exercise by asking students to write out their observations as full sentences or incorporate them into a full essay response.

This simple activity guides students to see essay writing as a fundamentally analytical task. That struggling students often find this revelatory only underlines the value of this activity.

Practising Prose

Fluent and sophisticated prose can seem effortless, a product not of sustained hard work but of natural ability. By contrast, we want our students to understand that great writing doesn't just happen—it is made. We want them to see how literary works of great complexity are built from simple parts … and we want students to recognise that hard work and an understanding of the mechanics of writing can help them find their own voice too.

These teaching strategies identify one key element of writing prose and offer a deliberative method for practising that skill in the everyday English classroom:

- The linking game helps students develop the vocabulary for weaving simple ideas into a complex cohesive response.
- Grouping evidence exercises encourage students to look for patterns in the text and provide a structure for fluently presenting that information. Quote-limit activities offer students a way to practise applying these skills.
- However-ing signals to students the importance of addressing complexity and contradiction in their essay writing.
- Developed reading exercises help students map the development of their own thinking.
- Teaching students to employ woven quotes offers them a more sophisticated way to present their insights.
- Line length activities help them present these insights in a more fluent fashion.
- Modelling techniques for comparing pieces of writing also aids the sophistication and fluency of their responses.
- Lastly, mastery grids offer teachers a fast, formative way to record students' progress as they master these writing skills and, in the process of becoming better writers, become better thinkers.

LINKING GAME

The best student answers not only make insightful observations about a text but also link these observations together in a cohesive and fluent fashion. The linking game is a quick and easy-to-facilitate activity that gives students an opportunity to practise this skill.

Instructions:
1. Have students write out a list of key themes or ideas of a particular poem, passage or text.
2. Then ask students to write a short paragraph in which they describe these basic themes in full sentences.
3. Now ask them to rewrite the paragraph for greater clarity and coherence by adding linking words and phrases from a list of examples:

Correspondingly	*Conversely*	*However*
Similarly	*Nevertheless*	*Furthermore*
By Contrast	*Consequently*	*Accordingly*

One engaging variation of this activity is to give students a list of observations about a text as well as a list of linking phrases and then challenge them to incorporate as many insights and observations into a single answer as possible. Collating insights from the class to create the list and getting students to highlight each phrase are useful strategies for ensuring students remain engaged throughout the task.

> The most effective student answers not only make insightful observations about a text but also link these observations together in a cohesive and fluent fashion.

GROUPING EVIDENCE

Grouping evidence—using multiple quotations in a single sentence—is a common feature of fluent essay writing.

> Here Auden creates a deflated sense of a world in retreat: everything and everyone 'rusted,' 'limp' and 'shrunk.'

This is an easy technique to teach and can substantially improve the quality of student responses relatively quickly. Teaching this rhetorical technique cues students to notice patterns within a piece of writing as well as encourages them to provide more plausible evidence for their arguments.

Below are two ways to help students learn and practise this skill.

Grouped Evidence Illustration Task

1. Give students a short extract or poem that vividly describes a setting.
2. Have students draw a quick sketch depicting this scene. Remind them that this task is not a test of their drawing skills and that you are really seeking that they convey some of the feeling or tone of the scene.
3. Get them to label the picture with short quotations (one or two words or some brief phrases) from the scene as evidence for their depiction.
4. Finally, ask your students to write a paragraph in which they group these quotes into a series of single sentences that conveys the tone of the scene.

Grouped Evidence Practice Task

1. Select a poem or passage of writing that is emblematic of one feature of a text (such as development of character, use of form, description of a key setting).
2. Ask students to write a four-sentence paragraph describing this passage or poem with the proviso that three of these sentences contain more than one short quote from the text.

> Wallace sketches a rural scene of 'butcher's grass', 'starlings' and 'insects all business all the time'. He deftly depicts a beautiful summer scene, all 'ale sunshine' and 'coins of sunlight', the 'horizon trembling' in the 'Am heat'. Wallace contrasts this 'very old land' with a constructed world that is only faintly registered—'the interstate' reduced to a 'shush'.

3. Share these sentences as a class, making a point of noting on the board the different techniques students employed for weaving quotes into their own writing.

4. You can then repeat the process with another passage. Some teachers use this second practice as an opportunity to have students trial at least one of the techniques for weaving quotations that have just been modelled on the board.

5. Students then repeat the process using the same passage but focusing on authorial style. This is an important step as it emphasises the point that we group evidence not to retell a story but to support our analysis. This exercise helps students not only recognise common features of the writer's style but also a structured way to present them to an audience.

> Wallace's passage is emblematic of his style. There are the exhaustively detailed list-like sentences: 'wild oat, vetch, butcher's grass' and 'quartz and chert and schist', which are then contrasted with short, punchy constructions such as 'NO HUNTING' and 'Sock's burrs'. He uses direct address to implore the reader ('Read' 'Look') to play close attention to these visual details. However, the use of sound is just as inventive, with the 'shush' of the interstate and the 'electric' noise of the insects.

Quote-Limit Activity

A quote-limit activity is an excellent way to test your students' ability to group their evidence at the end of a task, or to check their progress mid-task. Students are instructed to write an analytical text essay but with the twist that they must observe the following rules:

- They must support every assertion about the text with a quote.
- They must not quote more than thirty words from the text.

To do this successfully students must be able to employ quotes in a precise fashion. They must practise pointing out patterns in the text by grouping their evidence rather than quoting longer, more detailed examples.

Senior students who regularly use this technique become accomplished at sketching the tone or narrative of an entire scene in a handful of carefully chosen phrases:

> Fienberg describes Callisto's visit to the doctor as a 'disaster', a scene full of 'howls' and 'tears', her mouth falling open like 'crashing meteor's ... crater'.

DEVELOPED READING

A student's view of a text changes over the course of studying it.

Reading literature is a tentative, recursive process. Reading is really re-reading. Teaching students to map this ongoing process improves their overall reading of the text and gives them specific insights they can employ to great effect in their essays. An insight gained from this kind of 'developed' reading will add depth and complexity to their responses.

This technique has many labels: first and second impressions, the one-two punch and February–October paragraphs. However, the common feature of all developed reading techniques is teaching students to structure their analysis paragraphs to mirror how their view of the text has changed. They outline their initial impressions in the opening of the paragraph and then conclude with their more considered view:

> At first it seems like Elizabeth is particularly good at judging people's characters. However, we eventually realise that she too can be a victim of 'pride and prejudice'.

> Despite his warning, we initially accept Herbert Badgery's version of events. The reader soon becomes aware that he is not the most reliable narrator.

This approach is very simple but it can help create complex results:

> Initially, The English Patient seems a novel of broken lives and fractured stories. The English patient appears to be a haunted character, someone whose ordeals and injuries distance him from the world. We note the reserved manner of his speech and the formality of his manners. Hana is similarly haunted and at first is numb to everything but the tender intimacies of his care. Their shared reserve is echoed in the patient's standoffish behaviour when he first meets Katherine: observe the way Ondaatje subtly contrasts the distance between these two characters and the 'family' of the other figures on the expedition. However, our initial impressions are misleading—the English patient after all isn't even English. Both Hana and Almasy's stories are ones of passion: the intense grief of their respective losses, the redemptive possibility of falling in love. The novel is not a story of reserve but one of connection, of making a link between those around us and who we really are.

Indeed, while this might be a more detailed response than the other examples cited above, in terms of structure it is quite similar. The first impression of the character is presented and then challenged by a more developed reading. This technique neatly demonstrates what we want students to learn about essay writing: that complex, high-level responses are built out of a range of simple rhetorical strategies.

DEVELOPED READING TABLE

Asking students to compare their impressions of characters from the start of the text to those at the end is an effective deliberative practice exercise for honing this specific skill:

1. Ask students to discuss with a partner both their initial impression of a text's characters and what they think of this character by the end of the story. Log the results into a simple table like the one below.

CHARACTER	FIRST IMPRESSION	FINAL IMPRESSION
Mrs Bennet	Annoying. Only seems to care about her daughters getting married. Like lots of people in the society in which *P&P* is set she seems to be conscious of $ and class ('5000 a year'). Frustrated by her husband's jokes.	Still pretty frustrating but is worried for her daughters. (Understands what might happen to them in the world she lives in.) Mis-matched marriage.
Mr Bennet		
Darcy		

2. Ask students to then write a sentence summing up their first impression:

   Mrs Bennet is a frustrating character who embodies the worst values of the society Austen depicts.

3. Now get them to repeat the task, but this time including both their first and second impressions:

   Initially, the reader views Mrs Bennet as the embodiment of the worst values of the society Austen depicts. Eventually we come to see her as a victim of these values.

A good follow-up to this activity is to get students to integrate these short paragraphs into a longer piece of analysis such as an analytical text essay.

COMPARING PIECES OF WRITING

Teaching students to group quotes helps them draw a range of evidence from across a poem or passage. It can also be helpful to teach students how to explore links *between* different poems and passages. Drawing comparisons and noting contrasts between pieces of writing is a high-order skill that requires careful teaching and sustained practice, but a good starting point is to provide students with models of how this can be done. It is important here that these models identify specific techniques of comparison as this makes it far more likely that students will draw on these in their own writing.

> Drawing comparisons and noting contrasts between pieces of writing is a high-order skill.

Establish how character is explored across a range of scenes

The earnest Hermione Granger is always described as eager to do the right thing: reading all her books before the courses start, proud to be the first to levitate her feather, reluctant to follow Harry and Ron's rule-breaking schemes.

Use events in a particular scene to refer to the text's wider narrative

Ellie's actions here are typical of the growing courage that she and her friends demonstrate throughout the novel. Stepping from the darkness in this moment is not easy but her reluctance only emphasises her bravery. Indeed, this event in Chapter Seven foreshadows the strength and valour she demonstrates by the story's end, leading this group of brave young people.

Discuss particular narrative strategies employing examples from more than one scene

Winton's detailed descriptions of the room in the opening paragraphs ('coralline aggregations' of bird droppings, 'the grout-sick shower stall') describe Keely's world but also his state of mind. Winton employs this technique again and again: Keely reeling hungover in the heat of a summer day ('the street branding, blinding breath sucking' 'colours so saturated they were almost carcinogenic') or trying later to gulp down a meal from a 'malarial bain marie' at a run-down café.

Use similarities of theme to link your poem or passage to another

In 'Under Sirius', Auden comments on the fast-fading optimism and integrity of his era—much like the 'low, dishonest decade' of 'September 1st, 1939'.

Identify the tensions at play within the author's work citing multiple pieces of writing

In 'The Knight', 'Aunt Jennifer's Tigers' and 'Snapshots of a Daughter in Law', Adrienne Rich is preoccupied with the way gender can be both a prison and an identity through which to escape oppression. The tight, structured form of the first poems mirrors these limits while the freer verse of the latter echoes her protagonist's struggle to throw them off. Rich sees no easy answers in addressing these contradictions but is clear that she is seeking something that is 'delivered, palpable, ours'.

Where possible, address your topic sentences to the poem or whole text

The author's complex critique of gender inequality in marriage is a key feature of *The Tenant of Wildfell Hall*. Brontë's powerful portrayal and condemnation of the unequal status of husband and wife is explored in this chapter.

Discuss how form shapes meaning throughout the text

The long, digressive passages underline the character's intense self-involvement. Wallace juxtaposes these with brief interviews that also capture the fractured worldview of these characters, men disconnected from the world and alienated from themselves.

Explore a recurring symbol or motif of the text

Fitzgerald uses this image as a symbol of the elusive nature of the American Dream. From our first glimpse of Gatsby reaching for the green light in Chapter One to the image of it in Chapter Nine as an emblem of a new America, the light is a symbol of aspiration. An aspiration, we are told at the end of the novel, that Gatsby still believes in but one that tragically will always recede from him.

Asking students to seek out examples of these techniques in an editing Yahtzee activity (see page 76) is a natural next step for teachers wanting to encourage students to use the techniques in their own essay writing.

HOWEVER-ING

Another feature of high-level essay responses is that they show an awareness of the complexities and contradictions of texts. A classic technique for helping students avoid the trap of talking about text in a reductive or simplistic fashion is to devote some class time to 'however-ing'.

Instructions:

1. Ask students to write down a series of statements summarising their key views about the text.

   The characters in Romeo and Juliet are divided by bitter family rivalries.

   Mr Collins is totally consumed by his own social advancement.

2. Now ask them to list one instance where each of these broad assertions is not the case.

   However, some characters such as Prince Escalus and Friar Lawrence are able to avoid these petty disputes.

   However, he is, in his limited way, thinking of the Bennet sisters' welfare.

3. Using these statements, students can now write a short paragraph in which they discuss one or more of these broad assertions while also including reference to where they are contradicted or could be contested. Providing students with a list of phrases that help them word the acknowledgement of these contradictions in a fluent way makes this a more accessible task for students who might otherwise find this activity difficult.

This activity can also be used with essay topics. For instance, many students are trained to use simple question frames to analyse essay questions (e.g. Agree, Disagree & Also). *However-ing* is an effective alternative. Students sketch their basic response to a topic and then actively look for examples that challenge or undermine this point of view. They then revise their thesis. This concrete, evidence-led approach helps strengthen their argument in a way that students find intuitive and easy to apply. However-ing is both an excellent warm-up and follow-up activity to the line debate exercise on page 52.

LINE LENGTH ACTIVITIES

These *line length activities* are short, sharp activities that give students instant feedback on the extent of their sentence variation. This simple feedback loop cues students to be more conscious of the rhythm of their writing—an aspect of their practice of which they are often unaware. These activities work well for older or more able writers, and students often take real pleasure in the challenge of revising their sentences to avoid repeating the same sentence length.

0/10/20/30

One version of this activity involves dividing sentence structures into groups of tens: 0-9, 10-19, 20-29, 30-40. Students then have to write at least three paragraphs of a text analysis essay where no two adjoining sentences have the same approximate number of words. In this way, a long multi-clause sentence of thirty-two words can't be followed up with another sentence whose word length is in the thirties. Instead, a writer might pick a pithy quote or a shorter qualification of less than ten words:

> *Pride and Prejudice* explores the narrow expectations of behaviour that govern etiquette in Austen's England and the way some characters are able to move beyond 'these first impressions'. (27) Austen introduces these ideas in the opening scene. (8) Her ironic tone allows her to playfully explore the tragicomedy of those whose lives become consumed by conventional mores. (19) The 'universal truths' they act on are anything but ... (9)

Sentence Word Count

A *sentence word count* is a more challenging version of this style of activity. In it you ask your students to write an essay in which no sentence is of the same word length as another. Start the exercise by asking the class to write the numbers 4 to 36 down the margin column of their lined paper. There should be a numeral to the left of the margin on each line. Then, as they write the essay they should do two things to keep the count:

- At the end of each sentence add the number of words it contains in brackets. Like this. (2)
- Cross out the margin count to indicate that you can no longer use any more sentences of that length.

During the exercise students typically concentrate on the number of words per sentence, but at the end of the exercise they often note the way different sentence lengths improve the rhythm of their prose.

WOVEN QUOTES

NOTE: This is a technique that is most useful for older or more accomplished students.

Literary texts encompass a complex play of sophisticated ideas. Often students write about these ideas as though they are presented in a simple way:

> Auden's poetry is about indifference, cruelty and sometimes human connection.

Obviously, this 'laundry list' of themes does not sufficiently reflect the sophisticated concepts involved. There are many strategies that can be used to address this problem, but for able students the 'woven quote' technique—replacing thematic labels with quotes from the text that embody those themes —is an excellent way to create more depth and nuance in their response.

The first step for teaching this technique is asking students to simply add more detail to their response. In this way, more complex ideas are less likely to be reduced to a list of theme labels. For instance in Auden's work, a more detailed premise might read something like this:

> Auden's poetry paints a bleak picture of human failings. His poems explore tyranny, indifference and cruelty and are marked by brief moments of consolation. However, these times of respite only serve as ironic counterpoints to the bleak world of conformity and pain he depicts.

The next step is to get the student to qualify their premise. They can soften their language through modifiers and less absolute terms. Students can also employ qualifying clauses to their statements. This approach will better acknowledge the complex and sometimes contradictory manner in which ideas are presented in literature:

> Auden's poetry explores the *complex nature* of human *frailty*. He examines a world where, *without vigilance,* characters *can* drift into the lure of mindless hedonism or casual cruelty. This bleak vision is studded with moments of brief respite but *the fleeting connections and transitory pleasures* of his subjects only serve as an ironic counterpoint to the harsh realities of the world he describes.

Once a student response has reached this level of sophistication the 'woven quote' technique is very effective for creating an even more fluent essay. This is particularly useful as it is at this point that able students often plateau, writing detailed, thoughtful responses that nonetheless lack the sophisticated close reading of the very best essays. To employ a woven quote the student swaps the abstract concepts used in their response ('hedonism', 'human frailty') with quotes that embody these ideas. Obviously it takes practice to identify suitable quotes, but relatively quickly an able senior student will be able to start substituting an abstract label for a woven quote:

> Auden's poetry explores the complex nature of our 'false heart(s)'. He examines a world where characters are seduced by the 'Lie of Authority' or the hedonism of the 'sensual-man-in-the-street'. This bleak vision is studded with moments of brief respite, but the 'sweetness' of these consolations only serves as an ironic counterpoint to the harsh realities of the pervasive 'sorrow' he describes.

Getting the student to repeat the exercise using a different set of poems or passages but the same piece of their own writing is a good follow-up activity. In this way you can establish whether they have understood the underlying woven quotes technique.

> Auden's poetry explores the complex frailties of our 'faithless' natures. He examines the casual cruelty of 'Intendant Caesars' and the hedonistic who reduce everything to a 'mad camp.' This bleak vision is studded with moments of 'delight' but the brief respite of these moments only serves as an ironic counterpoint to the 'older, colder voice' of Auden's bleak world view.

Indeed some teachers take this follow-up activity a step further and have their students practise with a new text or poet to make sure they will be able to employ the technique beyond the context in which it was learned.

> In *Antigone*, Sophocles explores the tensions between 'the unwritten, unalterable laws of the Gods' and 'edicts' of the State. Despite Creon and Antigone embodying this tension, these ideas are never reduced to a simplistic dichotomy. Sophocles deftly sketches Creon's efforts to lead Thebes from 'trouble to tranquility' and how in the process he becomes 'a tyrant'. Similarly, the playwright's subtle and sympathetic portrait of Antigone positions the audience to empathise with her plight but also to understand how her 'stubborn spirit' contributes to her fate. Indeed it is the balance and moderation of the play's minor characters that Sophocles ultimately endorses.

A woven quote is the key feature of sophisticated close reading. Teaching students this specific skill is another instance where deliberative practice helps students see excellence not as something you are or aren't—but something that can be learned.

MASTERY GRID

In this chapter of *The Literature Toolbox* we have explored fourteen deliberative practice strategies for helping students refine their essay writing skills. A mastery grid is a powerful tool for organising these different strategies into a single, cohesive approach to teaching essay writing.

Clymer and Wiliam (2006) developed Mastery grids as a way of recording fine-scale data that students would find meaningful and teachers would find easy to collect. It was originally designed for science students but works particularly well in an English class. To make a mastery grid, teachers create a spreadsheet that identifies a series of skills that students must learn to attain mastery (see example on page 91). Teachers then keep an ongoing record of student skill acquisition using a simple scoring system:

2 = Strong evidence of mastery
1 = Some evidence of mastery
0 = No evidence of mastery

This simple feedback scheme has two substantial advantages for teaching essay writing. Firstly, it helps shift students from a task focus to a skills focus. Clymer and Wiliam found that this helped generate a more responsive, longer-term approach to learning. Students using a mastery grid tend to be more alive to incremental improvements in their work and the eventual goal to which they are headed. They are also aware that if they ignore an aspect of their writing or if their application drops off their mark can actually go down.

Secondly, this running record is easy to keep amidst the hectic demands of an everyday classroom. The three-point scale is quick to assess and lends itself to short, deliberative practice exercises focusing on a single skill. It is often used during periods of revision as it provides fast feedback on a specific task while reminding students of the overall scope of what they are trying to achieve. The fine-scale evidence can also be easily summarised for summative purposes. (For an overall percentage score, you simply multiply a ten-skill grid by five.)

In his book *Embedded Formative Assessment* (2011), Wiliam deftly summarised the advantages of this technique:

> Students became more engaged in monitoring their own learning; frequently asked for clarification, both from the teacher and their peers; and regarded the teacher more as a coach than a judge. Their achievement went up too.

This is an ideal tool for helping students understand how the different skills discussed in this chapter inform the complex craft of essay writing.

MASTERY GRID—ESSAY TECHNIQUE

	Contention Responds to Prompt	Organise Ideas in Paragraphs	Write a Conclusion	Employ Quotes	Analyse Quotes	Grouped Evidence	One Idea per Sentence	Link Ideas	Developed Reading	Proofing for Error
Amir										
Jack										
Liam N										
Abbey										
Ella										
David										
Jem										
Liam K										
Sophie										
Tao										
Tayah										
Devin										
Oki										
Aisha										
Sunny										
Noah										
Jack P										
Evie										
Class Average										
	Coherent Structure			Evidence				Fluency and Accuracy		

About the Author

Glen Pearsall is quite simply Australia's most dynamic and engrossing author and presenter on student engagement in the classroom."

Michael Victory, Teacher Learning Network

Glen Pearsall's reputation is built on his long record of bringing about real and lasting change in student behavior in both Primary and Secondary schools. He is Australia's most acclaimed educational consultant.

Miles Campbell, Teacher Training Australia

Glen was a Teacher Leader at Eltham High School and board member of the Victorian Curriculum Assessment Authority. He works throughout the world as an educational consultant, specialising in engaging instructional practice, student behaviour, feedback and assessment, differentiation, peer coaching and workload reduction for teachers.

Glen has been a Cambridge Education associate, a master class presenter for TTA and a research fellow at the Centre for Youth Research, University of Melbourne. Glen has a long association with the Teacher Learning Network and Critical Agendas and was the founding presenter of the widely popular PD in the Pub series. He is also co-creator of Toon Teach, an animated series on creating positive classrooms.

Glen is the author of the best-selling *And Gladly Teach* (2010), *Classroom Dynamics* (2012), *The Literature Toolbox* (2014), *Fast and Effective Assessment* (2019.) He is the co-author of *Literature for Life* (2005), *Work Right* (2011) and *Tilting Your Teaching* (2020). His ebook on questioning T*he Top Ten Strategic Questions for Teachers* (2013) was translated into Khmer for Cambodian teachers. Glen's latest project has been a collaboration with TTA to create argumentative AI avatars with whom teachers can practice their techniques for pivoting around arguments and de-escalating potential conflicts.

Glen can be contacted at Amba Press or via email at pearsallglen@gmail.

References

Beers, K. (2002). *When kids can't read: What teachers can do.* Heinemann.
Bernabei, G. (2005). *Reviving the essay: How to teach structure without formula.* Discover Writing Press.
Blau, S. (2003). *The literature workshop: Teaching texts and their readers.* Heinemann.
Brown, P. C., Roediger, H. L., & McDaniel, M. A. (2014). *Make it stick: The science of successful learning.* Belknap Press.
Bruns, C. V. (2011). *Why literature? The value of literary reading and what it means for teaching.* Continuum Publishing.
Cahill, H. (2008). *Learning partnerships: The use of poststructuralist drama techniques to improve communication between teachers, doctors and adolescents* [Unpublished doctoral dissertation]. The University Of Melbourne.
Cahill, H., & Pearsall, G. (2006). *Literature for life: Enhancing social and emotional literacy through the English curriculum.* Good Grief.
Clymer, J., & Wiliam, D. (2006). Improving the way we grade science. *Educational Leadership, 64*(4), 36–42.
Dean, C. B., Hubbell, E., Pitler, H., & Stone, B. (2012). *Classroom instruction that works: Research-based strategies for increasing student achievement* (2nd ed.). ASCD.
Dweck, C. S. (2006). *Mindset: The new psychology of success.* Random House.
Fish, S. (2011). *How to write a sentence: And how to read one.* Harper Collins.
Hattie, J. (2009). *Visible learning: A synthesis of over 800 meta-analyses relating to achievement.* Routledge.
Hutchinson, J., Ishler, M., & Wilen, W. (2000). *Dynamics of teaching.* Longman.
Jensen, E. (2001). *Arts with the brain in mind.* ASCD.
Johnson, T. D., & Louis, D. R. (1987). *Literacy through literature.* Methuen.
Madden, M. (2006). *99 ways to tell a story: Exercises in style.* Jonathon Cape.
Moretti, F. (2013). *Distant reading.* Verso.
Olsen, C. B. (2011). *The reading/writing connection: Strategies for teaching and learning in the secondary classroom,* Pearson.
Paivio, A. (2006). *Mind and its evolution: A dual coding theoretical approach.* Taylor and Francis.
Pearsall, G. (2010). *And gladly teach: A classroom handbook.* TLN Press.
Pearsall, G. (2012). *Classroom dynamics: A teacher's handbook.* TLN Press.
Pearsall, G. (2013). *The top ten strategic questions for teachers.* Free Ebook TTA/TLN Press.

Peterson, A. (2009, December 2). Cognitive skills development: An ELL success story gets NCTE award. *National Writing Project.* http://www.nwp.org/cs/public/print/resource/2992.

Pennebaker, J. W. (2011). *The secret life of pronouns: What our words say about us.* Bloomsbury.

Rowe, M. B. (1987). Wait time: Slowing down may be a way of speeding up! *American Educator, 11*(1), 38–43.

Smith, I. (2007). *Assessment and learning pocketbook.* Teachers' Pocketbooks.

Wilhelm, J. (2001). *Improving comprehension with think-aloud strategies: Modeling what good readers do.* Scholastic Professional Books.

Wiliam, D. (2011). *Embedded formative assessment.* Solution Tree.

Woods, J. (2008). *How fiction works.* Jonathon Cape.

Young, T. (2008). *Studying English literature: A practical guide.* Cambridge University Press.

Online Resources:

Project Zero Thinking Routines http://pzweb.harvard.edu

Ngram Viewer https://books.google.com/ngrams/

Index

Beers, Kylene, 8
Bernabei, Gretchen, 20
Blank prompts, 25
Blau, Sheridan, 8
Bundling swap, 69

Character ranking, 69
Cheat cheet scramble, 42-3
Clymer, Jacqueline, 90
Code words, 9, 32-3
Cold calling, 23
Comparing pieces of writing, 78, 84-5
Confidence test, 44
Connotations game, 12
Continuum activities, 52-3
Critical material auction, 54, 61
Cue sheets, 16

Developed reading, 78, 82-3
Distant reading, 27

Editing Yahtzee, 76
Elaboration cues, 24-25
Exacto, 42
Exampling, 26

Feedback, 12, 68, 87, 90
Feedback box, 72
Fish, Stanley, 8
Formative tests, 44
Foundation knowledge, 1, 37-8
Four corners, 53
Four tell, 45

Golden question, 24
Grouping evidence, 30, 78, 80-1

Hidden thoughts, 54, 56-7
Hot seat, 58-9
However-ing, 78, 86

Instant picture books, 40
Inverse models, 74-5
Inverted questions, 24

Johnson, Terry, 62

Line debating, 52-53
Line length activities, 78, 87
Linking game, 78-9
Literature trial, 59-60
Louis, Daphne, 62

Madden, Matt, 41
Mastery grid, 78, 90-1

Ngram Viewer, 27, 31
No glossing rule, 24
Non-linguistic representations, 62-63

Olsen, Carol Booth, 16
Open and closed quiz, 44
Open-book index challenge, 14-15

Pause time, 23-4
Placeholder statements, 25
Plot box, 42, 72
Project Zero, 20, 24, 96
Prompt generator, 47, 50-1

Question relay, 23
Quotation strips, 70-1
Quote-limit activity, 78, 81

Race the bell, 41
Reading process reports, 47, 48–49
Reflective statements, 25
Replacement tasks, 10–11
Rich questions, 24, 56
Role-play activities, 54, 58–60

Second draft, 26
See, think and wonder, 20–1
Sentence word count, 87
Sequence strips, 39
Silent screen/blank screen, 21
Sixteens, 77
Smith, Ian, 25
Sociograms, 62–3
Split-page analysis, 18–9
Student-composed revision test, 44
Support-challenge continuum, 12, 73
Synthesis tasks, 42–3

Testing foundation knowledge, 42
Three-colour highlighting, 8–9

Up and down game, 10, 46
Unpacking a sentence, 7–8

Venn diagrams, 63

Wait time, 23–4
Wilhelm, Jeffrey, 49
Wiliam, Dylan, 52, 90
Woods, James, 8
Word clouds, 28–30
Woven quotes, 78, 88–9

0/10/20/30, 87
70/30 Exam, 44

www.ingramcontent.com/pod-product-compliance
Lightning Source LLC
Chambersburg PA
CBHW050302120526
44590CB00016B/2462